Real Emotions
Real Devotions
Modern Psalms

Volume 1

By Lester Bailey

8 Owls
PUBLISHING
Voices of Wisdom, Redemption, and Kingdom Creativity

Dedication

"I bless GOD every chance I get; my lungs expand with His praise. I live and breathe GOD; if things aren't going well, hear this and be happy: Join me in spreading the news; together let's get the word out."

Psalm 34:1-3 MSG

I am continually amazed how God aligns and places the right people and the right skill sets in place to bring about something so out of the norm. The bizarre set of circumstances that led to this poetic devotion is nothing short of a genuine miracle. The list ranges from some who had no knowledge of the spark generated by a passing comment, compiling the continual verses coursing through my brain, the supportive family, and the seemingly benign friendships made during missionary trips that later proved invaluable to the project.

I pray blessings and shower my thankfulness to my friends:

To Pastor John Bates and the pastoral staff of Freedom Fellowship Int'l who prayed and nurtured an atmosphere of creativity and entrepreneurship, among other things.

To Sandy, my wife and high school sweetheart, for enduring the boyish excitement generated by the prospect of new arenas not even imagined before.

To our grown kids: Lydia, Kayla, Johnathan and Katie for your input and problem solving skills. Some of which are evident in the book.

To my nephew Brian Chapman who patiently took a four hour monologue and crafted the amazing cover illustration.

To Mike and Kristene O'Dell, my friends turned encouragers, ghostwriters, editors, and publishers.

I cannot and will not stand alone. Each added a piece to the picture of this devotional. I am thankful and humbled by each shade added to the vibrant color. I pray you enjoy the view.

Table of Contents

Modern Psalm 1: Loneliness — **page 1**
    Poem — page 2
    Practical Application — page 5
    Doodle Page — page 6

Modern Psalm 2: What About Me? — **page 7**
    Poem — page 8
    Practical Application — page 11
    Doodle Page — page 12

Modern Psalm 3: Creation Sings — **page 13**
    Poem — page 14
    Practical Application — page 17
    Doodle Page — page 18

Modern Psalm 4: Thanksgiving — **page 19**
    Poem — page 20
    Practical Application — page 23
    Doodle Page — page 24

Modern Psalm 5: Speaking Life — **page 25**
    Poem — page 26
    Practical Application — page 29
    Doodle Page — page 30

Modern Psalm 6: Peace — **page 31**
    Poem — page 32
    Practical Application — page 35
    Doodle Page — page 36

Modern Psalm 7: Creativity — **page 37**
    Poem — page 38
    Practical Application — page 41
    Doodle Page — page 42

Modern Psalm 8: The Word of God — **Page 43**
    Poem — page 44
    Practical Application — page 47
    Doodle Page — page 48

Modern Psalm 9: God's Blessing — **page 49**
    Poem — page 50
    Practical Application — page 53
    Doodle Page — page 54

Modern Psalm 10: Our Father — **page 55**
    Poem — page 56
    Practical Application — page 59
    Doodle Page — page 60

Modern Psalm 11: Dividing Walls — **page 61**
    Poem — page 62
    Practical Application — page 65
    Doodle Page — page 66

Modern Psalm 12: Growing Together — **page 67**
    Poem — page 68
    Practical Application — page 71
    Doodle Page — page 72

Table of Contents

Modern Psalm 13: Cleansing — **page 73**
    Poem — page 74
    Practical Application — page 77
    Doodle Page — page 78

Modern Psalm 14: — **page 79**
    Poem — page 80
    Practical Application — page 83
    Doodle Page — page 84

Modern Psalm 15: Rest — **page 85**
    Poem — page 86
    Practical Application — page 89
    Doodle Page — page 90

Modern Psalm 16: Morning Prayer — **page 91**
    Poem — page 92
    Practical Application — page 95
    Doodle Page — page 96

Modern Psalm 17: Our Daily Bread — **page 97**
    Poem — page 98
    Practical Application — page 101
    Doodle Page — page 102

Modern Psalm 18: Peacemakers — **page 103**
    Poem — page 104
    Practical Application — page 107
    Doodle Page — page 108

Modern Psalm 19: Abundant Life — **page 109**
    Poem — page 110
    Practical Application — page 113
    Doodle Page — page 114

Modern Psalm 20: Compassion — **Page 115**
    Poem — page 116
    Practical Application — page 119
    Doodle Page — page 120

Modern Psalm 21: Calling — **page 121**
    Poem — page 122
    Practical Application — page 125
    Doodle Page — page 126

Modern Psalm 22: Honor — **page 127**
    Poem — page 128
    Practical Application — page 131
    Doodle Page — page 132

Modern Psalm 23: Living Water — **page 133**
    Poem — page 134
    Practical Application — page 137
    Doodle Page — page 138

Modern Psalm 24: Fruitfulness — **page 139**
    Poem — page 140
    Practical Application — page 143
    Doodle Page — page 144

Introduction

Right smack in the middle of your Bible is a collection of songs sung to God that express the human condition in every season. This section is known as the Book of Psalms. The Psalms were written by people voicing their need for God. You will see the writers cry out to Father in the midst of praise, grief, betrayal, lack, and fear. These songs span the historical time frame of the Israelites under the Old Covenant beginning with Moses and ending with the time known as post-exilic (or, after their exile).

Obviously, our culture has changed over time. The things you face in this season stem from a different set of cultural values. However, the principles found in the Bible are eternal. They are what the human heart is in need of regardless of the times in which we are born.

This devotional is written in the style of a modern psalm book. It is a resource for you to process through the real fears, frustrations, and emotions that have surfaced because of our current circumstances. Each modern psalm is a prophetic word picture received through prayer for this purpose. A Biblical example has been added to each day's devotional so that you might see the struggles you face are common to mankind–but also to show that Jesus has the answer you are seeking. You then have been given a time of personal reflection through prayer and doodling so that you might process through your own spiritual and emotional needs.

Jesus is real! And He is not afraid of you being real with Him. As a matter of fact, that is what it means to have an authentic relationship with Jesus. You can talk to Him like He is your best friend. Do you know why? –because He is!

Modern Psalm 1: Loneliness

"Perfume and incense bring joy to the heart, and the pleasantness of a friend springs from their heartfelt advice."
Proverbs 27:9, NIV

I pant. I groan. I feel so alone.
Those I thought were close have left me and gone.

I wonder at night why I am here
and draw myself inward to a place of no cheer.

I begin to ask God why I'm in this place
and remember with fondness the times of His grace.

The heaviness is lifting and
I find myself yearning
for a contact of friendship of someone discerning.

One to draw strength from and encourage with laughs,
I begin to see sunlight
Now, to move from the past.

A group of several
perhaps over tea or a meal,
and I find myself moving to a place where I feel Your Goodness and Love.

I feel You so close.
You always lead me where I need You the most.

You Lord send love to help when I'm low,
to show me you care wherever I go.

I can now share
the love that You've sent
to someone I know who is broken or bent.

I have been lifted so I can now lift
another I see is just where I've been.

Your goodness Lord is greater than I can express
To give what I've gotten brings peace to my mess

Loneliness is an effective tool the enemy of our soul uses against us. Isolation can be a dangerous place. Our minds begin to react to scenarios, whether real or imagined, and the thought of negative possibilities can lead to self-destructive mindsets and actions.

Look up Genesis 2:18. God Himself said that it was not _____ for man to be alone.

Adam had fellowship with God. But Father in His wisdom knew that Adam needed someone who was like him. He needed fellowship with both God and other people. So, Father made Adam a partner with whom he could share his life.

We all need people in our lives who will encourage us, listen to us when we need to talk, speak the truth to us when we are struggling, and pray for us. King David was a man who sought after God with his whole heart. But, even so, Father knew that David would need a friend.

> *"As soon as he had finished speaking to Saul, the soul of Jonathan was knit to the soul of David, and Jonathan loved him as his own soul. And Saul took him that day and would not let him return to his father's house. Then Jonathan made a covenant with David, because he loved him as his own soul. And Jonathan stripped himself of the robe that was on him and gave it to David, and his armor, and even his sword and his bow and his belt. And David went out and was successful wherever Saul sent him, so that Saul set him over the men of war. And this was good in the sight of all the people and also in the sight of Saul's servants."*
> *1 Samuel 18:1-5, ESV*

The story of David and Jonathan describes one of the greatest friendships in the Bible. It wasn't a casual friendship. It was built upon a love for God's will and strengthened through adversity.

Look up Proverbs 17:17. What does it say about friendships formed for God's purposes?

Notice what took place between them. Jonathan made a covenant with David. This word for covenant meant that an alliance was formed between the two. They made an agreement that they would support, encourage, and defend one another. This was significant because Jonathan should have inherited the throne from his father King Saul, but he knew God was giving that honor to David. And notice that it was Jonathan who initiated the covenant. This showed great surrender to God's will and loyalty to David's future dynasty. Jonathan is a friend who displays great character–the kind that David would need to surround himself with if he were to be successful as king.

Proverbs 27:17 (NIV) says, *"As iron sharpens iron, so one person sharpens another."*

A great nugget of wisdom is this: If you recognize in your character something you'd like to see changed, gravitate toward believers who are strong in that area. By doing so, you will find a shift in that direction in yourself. It may come as a light bulb moment or gradually, but the shift will come.

If it's shyness, then surround yourself with extroverts. If you desire to be more generous, hang around givers and watch closely how God uses them.

In order to have these types of friends, you should seek to be that friend. The lessons you have learned in your life are valuable to others. Your collection of life experiences and growth in the things of God uniquely qualifies entrance into a sphere of people others cannot reach.

Paul teaches in Philippians 1:12 that the things he experienced in his life served to advance the Gospel. Use your past to direct someone else's future toward the good things God has for them, and for you.

Practical Application

List some ways others have helped you grow.

List some areas of your life you can use to help others

GOD IS LOVE

Modern Psalm 2: What About Me?

"Do nothing out of selfish ambition or vain conceit. Rather, in humility value others above yourself."
Philippians 2:3, NIV

This one is mine; you go get your own!
Immediately I feel my heart turn to stone.

I can feel my expression turn for the worst,
and the heartbeat inside is nearly a burst.

A snarky reply doesn't help to repulse,
the heaviness inside that is feeling so gross.

I try to give thanks for what I have grabbed,
the fake smile I show just can't hide the drab.

The cancer is growing and now I can see,
relationships suffer 'cause that's how I feel.

But you Lord have blessed me and all around I see,
the many things and friendships You've given to me.

I ache to be in Your presence and mend that distance I have created.
I know Lord You are trying to say release that thing, just give it away.

I give it with gladness to someone in need,
and lo and behold I suddenly see,
not just another, or two, but several of "that thing!!"

I now realize Your blessings just say,
"When you have abundance, just give it away".

Your Kingdom advances when Your blessings extended,
reaches a hand that is empty or a heart that's offended.

We arrive here on God's green earth with our own needs and wants foremost in our mind. We've all seen very small children exclaim "MINE!!" over something. We have also seen some who, although adult in stature, act in a similar fashion–much to the chagrin of those closest to them.

We, or at least I, have also witnessed relatively close relationships suffer because of my actions concerning "stuff."

Look up Galatians 6:7, MSG

"Don't be misled: No one makes a fool of God. What a person _____, he will harvest. The person who plants selfishness, ignoring the needs of others (ignoring God) will harvest a crop of weeds. All he'll have to show for his life is weeds! But the one who _____ in response to God, letting God's Spirit do the growth work in him, _____ a crop of real life, eternal life."

My selfish attitudes drew my focus inward, and hindered closeness with both God and those nearest to me. Conversely, I've learned that those who give freely, not only of the Lord's tithe but in all other areas, open up a fountain of blessing that continues to flow.

> *"A man was going down from Jerusalem to Jericho when he was attacked by robbers. They stripped him of his clothes, beat him, and went away leaving him half dead. A priest happened to be going down the same road, and when he saw the man, he passed by on the other side. So too a Levite, when he came to the place and saw him, passed by on the other side. But a Samaritan, as he traveled, came where the man was; and when he saw him, he took pity on him. He went to him and bandaged his wounds, pouring on oil and wine. Then he put the man on his own donkey, brought him to an inn, and took care of him. The next day, he took out two denarii and gave them to the innkeeper. 'Look after him,' he said, 'and when I return, I will reimburse you for any extra expense you may have.'"*
> Luke 10:30-35

Gal 5:16-18, MSG says: *"My counsel is this: Live freely, animated and motivated by God's Spirit. Then you won't feed the compulsions of selfishness. For there is a root of sinful self-interest in us that is at odds with a free spirit, just as the free spirit is incompatible with selfishness. These two ways of life are antithetical, so that you cannot live at times one way and at times another way according to how you feel on any given day. Why don't you choose to be led by the Spirit and so escape the erratic compulsions of a law-dominated existence?"*

Case in point: I like a particular brand of athletic shoe that starts at over $100.00. My first few pair I received as gifts. However, the first pair I bought myself, I kept in a box in the closet. While hosting a small group in our home, someone commented on the poor quality of their shoes. I felt a tug from Holy Spirit and found out this person's shoe size matched mine. I brought out my treasured box and offered it to them. They replied with an incredulous look and an attempt to refuse the gift saying, "This is just too much." Eventually the shoes were accepted, and a feeling of relief and gratitude came over me because Father had given me an opportunity to bless someone.

Fast forward a few months: As I thought about this particular story for this devotion, I looked in my closet. I now have six pair of those same shoes in a variety of colors. I've found them on clearance racks and received some as gifts. This is the return blessing of my obedience.

I have seen the same thing with $100 bills. My first "Pentecostal handshake" was scary because that amount was half of my paycheck. I had babies at home expecting to eat. But, I was obedient, and soon realized that I usually had a bill stuck somewhere to give. Now, over twenty years later, seldom do I not have at a $100 bill waiting to bless someone. The Lord knows that He can send me to those in need. Guitars, clothes, time, food–nothing is exempt from this promise. But the most amazing thing is, the gift often opens the door to speak life into someone's situation.

Practical Application

Have you ever been prompted by Holy Spirit to give something away that is valuable to you? Have you ever received something of value from someone who met your immediate need? Write it out.

How does it make you feel when you obey God, even if it seems hard at the time? Do you easily receive from others when God wants to bless you?

Modern Psalm 3: Creation Sings

"The Heavens declare the glory of God; the skies proclaim the work of His hands."
Psalm 19:1, NIV

Creation awaits the dawn of each day.
The birds greet with song the first of the rays.

Trees, arms extended, wave to approve,
and waves crash on rocks they are trying to move.

Weather and currents are given direction
by the finger of God without hesitation.

Flora and fauna attend to each day
the life You've extended each step of the way.

By word You created planets and stars,
we've given them names like Jupiter or Mars.

Yet on man You have given a special distinction,
a place near Your heart that follows Your reason.

Created for closeness with the One on the throne,
we're given a will we each call our own.

The rocks will cry out if we fail to praise
the Creator of heaven on our given day.

I'll take my position, my God the Most High,
to praise and honor You all of my life.

The more that I praise, the closer I feel
to the steps of Your throne, before You I kneel.

Your Spirit will change me each time we are near,
my motives more pure, the mission more clear.

To reach those hurting or weak or dismayed,
pointing to Jesus a more perfect way.

Did you know that all of creation is designed to sing praises to God? Adoration and joy are the currency of heaven. We can experience the atmosphere of heaven even now through the deposit made in us by Holy Spirit.

Look up 2 Corinthians 1:21-22, BSB

"Now, it is God who establishes both us and you in Christ. He anointed us, placed His seal on us, and put His Spirit in our hearts as a _____ of what is to come."

The word used for pledge in the New Testament means: a large part of the payment, given in advance as a security that guarantees the whole will be paid afterwards. The indwelling of the Holy Spirit brings with it many benefits that guarantee eternal life and the things of salvation. When we experience the fruit of the Spirit–which is the character of Holy Spirit–we experience the heart of God. We bring glory and honor to our Father when we walk in like manner being empowered by Holy Spirit to do so. Our faith doesn't just consist of the head knowledge of things pertaining to salvation, but rather it includes a choice we make to walk in step with the eternal things deposited within us. This requires that we let go of our own way of doing things and take hold of God's ways.

> *"I will extol the Lord at all times; His praise will always be on my lips. I will glory in the Lord; let the afflicted hear and rejoice. Glorify the Lord with me; let us exalt His name together. I sought the Lord and He answered me; He delivered me from all my fears. Those who look to Him are radiant; their faces are never covered with shame. This poor man called, and the Lord heard him; He saved him out of all his troubles. The angel of the Lord encamps around those who fear him, and he delivers them.*
> *Psalm 34:1-7, NIV*

King David wrote Psalm 34 as he was running for his life. It is easy for us to paint a picture of David full of faith, with sword drawn, never giving himself over to a feeling of desperation or fear. But that's not what he says. Instead, he encourages others who are experiencing affliction and hardship to learn the faith lessons that got him through his own trials and difficulties. His advice? – glorify God by praising Him in the midst of uncertainty and fearful situations.

Listen, spiritual warfare is real. We all face the temptation to be drawn away from the reality of God's goodness when we experience fearful or painful situations. The enemy's goal is to get us so focused on our difficulty that we behave in a manner more in line with his ways instead of tapping into the eternal deposit of the Kingdom within us. This is the faith battle that every believer will face. It is precisely in these moments, when we don't feel like praising God, that we should seek Him in this manner. Why? Because praise connects us back to the reality of heaven. It reminds us that we no longer belong to this world but are citizens of another. As true sons and daughters of the King, we have been given authority over the enemy. Our praise to God allows for Holy Spirit to strengthen us to walk in our God given authority and to gain victory over that which is coming against us.

God doesn't just want you to sing to Him. He wants you to win the battles you face. He is the source of the victory. When we praise Him during affliction, we are saying our faith is resting upon His goodness toward us in our circumstances. The devil has no answer to that kind of faith. He loses every time.

In light of what we just talked about, read the following scriptures and think about what they mean.

- *"'I tell you,"He replied, "If they keep quiet, the stones will cry out.'" Luke 19:40, NIV*
- *"The heavens declare His righteousness, and all the peoples see His glory." Psalm 97:6, AMPC*
- *"Who can hide in secret places so that I cannot see them?" declares the Lord. "Do not I fill heaven and earth?" declares the Lord." Jeremiah 23:24, NIV*
- *"Come, let us sing for joy to the Lord; let us shout aloud to the Rock of our salvation." Psalm 95:1, NIV*
- *"I remain confident of this: I will see the goodness of the Lord in the land of the living." Psalm 27:13, NIV*

Practical Application

What is your tendency when you face a difficult situation? Be honest with yourself. Are you prone to anger, fear, despondency, or avoidance? Write out your thoughts.

Has this idea of Holy Spirit as a down payment of the joyful atmosphere of heaven changed the way you will tap into the help He offers when you face temptation?

FIND ME!
JONAH4

Modern Psalm 4: Thanksgiving

"Be anxious for nothing, but in everything by prayer and supplication, with thanksgiving, let your requests be made known to God; and the peace of God, which surpasses all understanding, will guard your hearts and minds through Christ Jesus."
Philippians 4:6-7, NKJV

I waken at night, I sing praises!

The beginning of light, I sing praises!

*Kids in the car, going near, going far,
wherever we are I sing praises!*

It's Thursday, no cash, I sing praises!

The car needs some gas, I sing praises!

*There's a knock at the door,
"I've just been to the store, and I've got so much more ..."
I sing praises!!*

My wallet is stuffed, I sing praises!

I have more than enough, I sing praises!

*I can see that you're down and no one's around,
I'll share what we have, I sing praises!*

*You may see in this phrase there is POWER IN PRAISE
and will lengthen your days
Just sing praises!*

Building on our previous lesson concerning praise, let's look at what having an attitude of gratitude does for our spiritual, emotional, and physical health.

Anxiety and depressive disorders are much more common in young adults than in past generations. High school and college students are five times more likely to suffer from depression and anxiety compared to teenagers fifty years ago. Social isolation and loneliness are some of the biggest issues that a young adult who is depressed may experience. This can lead to many outcomes, including an individual feeling isolated and helpless on a regular basis.

There are numerous types of anxiety disorders, many of which have their own specific symptoms. Common issues are listed below, along with a short description of each.

> Generalized anxiety disorder consists of excessive and persistent worry about events, sometimes routine ones. The worry is above and beyond what is warranted and is difficult to control. This type of anxiety often coincides with these specifically named:
- Agoraphobia is an anxiety disorder that is characterized by a fear and avoidance of places and situations that may cause the person to feel panicked, trapped, or embarrassed.
- Panic disorder is a repeated episode of sudden intense anxiety that reaches a peak in a few minutes. This may cause shortness of breath, pounding heart, chest pain, or the feeling of being overwhelmed.
- Social anxiety disorder occurs when someone has high levels of anxiety which results in an avoidance of social situations. An individual will become reclusive as they feel self-conscious, embarrassed, or are worried about being viewed in a negative light.

https://peaksrecovery.com/blog/depression-anxiety-young-adults

Although anxiety may be on the rise, it is not new. Paul addressed anxiety in his letter to the Philippian church. *"Do not be anxious about anything, but in every situation, by prayer and petition, with thanksgiving, present your requests to God. And the peace of God, which transcends all understanding, will guard your hearts and your minds in Christ Jesus."* Philippians 4:6-7, NIV

The Greek word used for anxious in Paul's letter to the Philippians is **merimnaó**. It means a feeling of being pulled apart, divided, or something that is being pulled in opposite directions.

> *"Light is sweet, and it pleases the eyes to see the sun. However many years anyone may live, let them enjoy them all. But let them remember the days of darkness, for there will be many. Everything to come is meaningless. You who are young, be happy while you are young, and let your heart give you joy in the days of your youth. Follow the ways of your heart and whatever your eyes see but know that for all these things, God will bring you into judgment. So then, banish anxiety from your heart and cast off the troubles of your body, for youth and vigor are meaningless."*
> Ecclesiastes 11:7-10, NIV

The words above are written by the man said to be wiser than anyone in his day. When Solomon was crowned as king, he asked God for wisdom to rule rightly. That request pleased God and He granted wisdom and wealth to David's successor. However, when reading Ecclesiastes, we need to understand that at some point King Solomon became jaded in his thinking. He makes the statement in the beginning of Ecclesiastes that *"with much wisdom, comes much sorrow"* (Ecc 1:18). The Hebrew word **ka'ac** is the word used for sorrow. It is the same word used for anxiety in chapter 11. It actually means vexation, anger, or emotional pain, often initiated by the actions of others.

At the time that Solomon writes Ecclesiastes, he is having somewhat of an existential crisis. He concludes that the only thing that matters is finding a sense of enjoyment about life. However, it can't be found "under the sun." That means that peace can only be found in its heavenly source "above the sun." Jesus is the Prince of Peace, and His kingdom consists of righteousness, peace, and joy in the Holy Spirit (Romans 14:17). His desire is to bring a sense of wholeness to our lives so that we can live the abundant life only found in Him.

As believers, we choose the ways of peace by living in an attitude of thanksgiving and praise. We are certain to face trials of many kinds but, when we learn to bring God praise and thanksgiving in every situation, we begin to walk in authority over the things that cause anxiety and sorrow in our lives. Anxiety is real! And it can be immobilizing. Seek help and choose healthy habits. But know that Jesus wants to bring you into a place of peace and wholeness. It is His heart for every believer, no matter the struggle.

Practical Application

Praise is such an important part of our relationship with God. It focuses our attention on Him and not the situation. He has everything in hand and will extend blessings given to share. What situation do you need to praise Him over instead of worrying about?

"Thank [God] in everything [no matter what the circumstances may be, be thankful and give thanks], for this is the will of God for you [who are] in Christ Jesus [the Revealer and Mediator of that will]." 1 Thessalonians 5:18, AMPC

How can you reword your worries into praise?

FIND ME..
JONAH
4

Modern Psalm 5: Speaking Life

"Let the words of my mouth and the meditation of my heart be acceptable in Your sight, O Lord, my Rock and my Redeemer."
Psalms 19:14, ESV

As I sit here and ponder, my mind will soon wander
to things that might bring dismay.
Thoughts and emotions, weird or strange notions,
topics which lead to decay.

Talks with some people that carried much deeper
than acquaintances should venture to share.

I watch through my tea glass, the tiki torch flame
that's supposed to keep insects away,
And ponder the answer that Abba would fashion
to questions I'm asking today.

'Count it all joy' burns from my core
to troubles that May come my way.

"Speak blessings and life, not trouble and strife,"
I hear my good Father say.
You Lord give wisdom to any who hear You,
and this Lord I'm asking today.

A soft answer turns anger and be kind to strangers,
They'll know by the love that you show
That you're My disciple,
My peace I will give you, extend that wherever you go.

My heart now is burning, spirit is churning,
lurching an ache to release Jesus inside.

"Speak life" is the cry from my lips as I enter the street.

Words are powerful. God spoke and the earth was formed. The sound waves and vibrations that were sent forth from His creative voice were all that was needed in order to bring life out of nothing. Because we are created in God's image, our words hold weight as well. We don't have the ability to create out of nothing, but the words we use, and the inflection behind them, do create the atmosphere around us. We either partner with the Kingdom by speaking words of life, or we agree with the ways of a spiritually darkened world.

This is true for our thought life as well. We create the state of our mental and emotional well-being by the words we meditate upon. The words we speak are a direct result of what we have been allowing to take root in our minds and hearts. As we speak these words out, we reinforce the realm in which the ideas represent.

Look up 2 Corinthians 5:20, NIV
"We are therefore Christ's _____, as though God were making His appeal through us. We implore you on Christ's behalf: Be reconciled to God."

Merriam-Webster defines an ambassador as: a diplomatic agent of the highest rank accredited to a foreign government or sovereign as the resident representative of his or her own government or sovereign or appointed for a special and often temporary diplomatic assignment.

When we are saved, we are delivered from the domain of darkness and transferred into the Kingdom of Light (Colossians 1:13). We are then assigned as Ambassadors for Christ in this world to light the way for others to see the true Kingdom through both our words and our actions.

The problem lies in the fact that we are not yet fully sanctified. We still operate out of what we know. Our human tendency is to focus on the problems and challenges of life in a negative way. We diminish the light of the Kingdom through complaints and words of unbelief as we seek solutions to our needs through our own logic or experiential understanding. Make no mistake, we are representing a specific worldview when we operate as such, we are just not fulfilling our role as Christ's Ambassador.

The Greek word used in Paul's letter to the Corinthian church is ***presbeuó***. It too means to act as an established statesman (diplomat)–a trusted, respected ambassador who is authorized to speak as God's emissary. But it also has this element in its definition: an older, venerated person; or one who is mature.

> *"Now a Jew named Apollos, a native of Alexandria, came to Ephesus. He was an eloquent man, competent in the Scriptures. He had been instructed in the way of the Lord. And being fervent in spirit, he spoke and taught accurately the things concerning Jesus, though he knew only the baptism of John. He began to speak boldly in the synagogue, but when Priscilla and Aquila heard him, they took him aside and explained to him the way of God more accurately."*
> Acts 18:24-26, ESV

Apollos was a great speaker and teacher when it came to the scriptures. But notice that he needed to understand the ways of God in a more mature way. This new understanding most likely happened through being baptized in the Holy Spirit since it is noted that he had only known John's baptism. Why is that important? Because we cannot know the ways of the Kingdom unless we are governed internally by the Spirit. And our maturity level is clearly displayed for all to see through the way we use our words.

Paul says it this way, *"Be wise in the way you act toward outsiders (those yet to come into the Kingdom); make the most of every opportunity. Let your conversation be always full of grace (God's favor expressed through the empowerment of the Holy Spirit), seasoned with salt (that which spurs others on toward righteousness), so that you may know how to answer everyone."* Colossians 4:5-6, NIV.

Time taken to speak with our Father, and more importantly to listen as He speaks to us, will open you up to wholesale changes in your perspective. If we are going to represent the Kingdom, we need to be governed by the Spirit. That happens as we spend time with God through prayer and worship. We grow in maturity as we surrender to God in difficult situations instead of complaining and grumbling. James says this, *"Allow perseverance to finish its work, so that you may be mature and complete, not lacking in anything. Now if any of you lacks wisdom, he should ask God, who gives generously to all without finding fault, and it will be given to him. But he must ask in faith, without doubting, because he who doubts is like a wave of the sea, blown and tossed by the wind..."* James 1:4-6, NIV.

Practical Application

Read James 1:1-4. Identify the areas you know you need to mature in when it comes to the way you use your words. Ask God for wisdom in those areas and then be aware when you are put in situations that require you to change the way you have always responded.

Read Proverbs 15:1, Matthew 25:35, and John 13:35. Explain how responding to situations with these Kingdom principles shows that you are an Ambassador of Christ.

Praise God

FIND ME
Jonah 4

Modern Psalm 6: Peace

"Whoever seeks to preserve his life will lose it, but whoever loses his life will keep it."
Luke 17:33, ESV

Oh, for a moment's rest, Oh, for a moment's peace
I'm busy, I'm rushing, I can see no ease.

I think of a hamster on one of those wheels,
always the running, always uphill.

My mind is consumed with this thing or that,
and dreams are a mixture of chaos and wrath.

I try something numbing to give me an edge,
my body is hurting and so is my head.

"You seem so peaceful "I hear myself say
to one they call Christian I see every day.

"I've been where you've been, but I found new life
when I began serving the Lord Jesus Christ "

I feel something stirring inside as I spout
"That sounds intriguing," I know there's my out.

Our talks are more frequent, and I can now say
I'm firmly established where some call "the way".

I see myself changing,
I followed advice
and I began serving the Lord Jesus Christ.

My life is still busy but somehow I've found
there's peace in the chaos, I'm charting new ground.

Now I'm the one reaching to those who I see need
the peace in their chaos, "it's Jesus, you see."

Life can be busy and become entirely consuming. Personal agendas and goals easily take the place of our true purpose which is to bring honor and praise to God–the Creator of the Universe. Both our physical frailty and our drive to succeed often lead to the use of outside stimulants or depressants as a coping mechanism. This seems to keep us going for a bit, but the disruption of the natural cycle of rest, work, and play inevitably takes its toll. After a while, our inability to get a handle on our situations and circumstances often spiral into a place where we feel totally out of control.

However, our God is so loving and faithful to continually call us back to the place of rest only found in Him. Often, He does so through His people–others who have experienced His healing and can show us the way of escape from our hopeless attempts of bringing meaning to our lives apart from an abiding relationship with Father.

We begin to tap into our divine purpose when we first spend time with God; and second, seek to serve others. When asked what the greatest commandment was, Jesus said exactly those words, *"You shall love the Lord your God with all your heart and with all your soul and with all your mind."* Matthew 22:37, ESV. True peace and purpose in our lives stems from this understanding.

> *"Abide in Me, and I in you. As the branch cannot bear fruit of itself unless it abides in the vine, so neither can you unless you abide in Me. I am the vine, you are the branches; he who abides in Me and I in him, he bears much fruit, for apart from me you can do nothing."*
> John 15:4-5, ESV

The Greek word used for abide in this passage is **menó**. It means to remain, to wait, or to be continually present. Father desires that we abide in Him continuously. This doesn't come naturally to us. We tend to make our own way during the week in an attempt to accomplish what needs to be done and then we come to church on Sunday mornings to worship God. But this is not the complete definition of worship. Worship is not just an experience we have, but rather a posture of our heart. If our hearts are postured to live in the awareness of God's presence every day, and we seek His leading in our lives through prayer, we learn what it means to abide in Him. We then live out of the ways of the Kingdom, instead of needing to forge our own way in the world. One way brings life, peace, and joy–even in the midst of difficulty. The other tends to cause a sense of fracture and unrest in our souls.

Look up Matthew 11:29, NIV
"Take my yoke upon you and learn from me, for I am gentle and humble in heart, and you will find _____ for your souls."

The Greek word for rest in this verse is ***anapausis***. It means cessation from labor, recreation, or a temporary respite of soldiers. Why would this word be likened to the kind of rest that soldiers need? Because the rest that God gives brings peace to our inner turmoil. Biblical peace is not defined as an absent of troubling circumstances, but rather a sense of wholeness within even in the midst of those troubling circumstances.

The Hebrews had a word they used for peace–*shalom*. When they would enter or leave someone's home, they would speak a blessing over their hosts. That blessing was, ***"Shalom."*** In other words, "May your soul be at rest."

The NAS Old Testament Hebrew Lexicon defines *shalom* in this way:

1. completeness, soundness, welfare, peace
    a. completeness (in number)
    b. safety, soundness (in body)
    c. welfare, health, prosperity
    d. peace, quiet, tranquility, contentment
    e. peace, friendship
    f. of human relationships
    g. with God especially in covenant relationship
    h. peace (from war)
    i. peace (as adjective)

It is true that we will face spiritual warfare in our Christian walk. But Father wants us to learn to overcome the warfare and live in His welfare. The life that Jesus came to give us is abundant and full of peace and joy. Our world, however, is always in a state of unrest. The amount of peace we obtain in our lives is a direct result of whether or not we learn to abide in Christ. The question becomes how much "shell shock" do we want to live with by hanging on to our own ways of doing things instead of learning to take on the rest that is ours in Jesus.

Practical Application

Look up Matthew 11:28-30. Identify what you are yoked with (bound by) that causes unrest and trouble in your soul. Pray and tell Father that you want His yoke in this area of your life that will bring about His rest and peace.

Look up John 14:27. Jesus blessed His disciples as He was readying Himself to leave this world. He blessed them with, "Peace (or Shalom)." What is one tangible way you can take hold of this blessing that Jesus spoke over those who would be His disciples (both then and now)?

FIND ME!

Modern Psalm 7: Creativity

"And God saw everything that He had made, and behold, it was very good. And there was evening and there was morning, the sixth day."
Genesis 1:31, ESV

I see shapes in the clouds as plain as can be:
A dolphin, a puppy, a cat, a teepee.

There's tulips and sailboats and angels galore,
and faces of people I've seen at the store.

I can't help but praise You when I see all that.
A deepness inside me begins to reflect.
All the good things You've given I dare not reject.

Then a soft whisper, it seems, in my ear,
Says, "Blessings upon you year after year."

To say simply "Thank you" seems empty and base
when I am so grateful of Your mercy and grace.

I honor You Father for You are profound.
My spirit wells praises that lips can't expound

When God created mankind, He made us in His image. That means we have attributes which are similar to His. Certainly, we are not omniscient, or all powerful, but our need to create and be productive stems from God's image stamped within. The very first character trait we learn about God is that He is creative. He molded and shaped a world where life of all kinds could be sustained. He built layers of eco-systems that could not have just happened by chance. He paired the animal world with the proper vegetation. He placed just the right gravitational pull on the earth to create an atmosphere conducive for life. He hung the stars in the night canopy of the sky. He expressed His appreciation for beauty throughout the landscape of the nations. And, in His wisdom, He placed man in the garden to care for His handiwork with the understanding that Adam and Eve's curiosity for knowledge was inherent because of His likeness.

This creative bent is evident within us. When humanity is at our best, we build; we explore. We have the ability to change our environment. We learn how to create tools to be more productive in our work. We are inquisitive, artistic, musical, always reaching, always expanding. This is our basic toolset–a mind looking to expand. Father knew we needed this creativity to fulfill our mandate of having dominion over the earth.

God delights in renewing this sense of creativity within us, especially when it comes to fulfilling our God-given purpose. We are empowered by Holy Spirit to live in the creative expression that is needed to do that which Father asks of us. We see that all throughout the Bible. It is not just a New Testament idea.

> *"See the Lord has called by name Bezalel the son of Uri, son of Hur, of the tribe of Judah; and He has filled him with the Spirit of God, with skill, with intelligence, with knowledge, and with all craftsmanship, to devise artistic designs, to work in gold and silver and bronze, in cutting stones for setting, and in carving wood, for work in every skilled craft."*
> *Exodus 35:30-33, ESV*

Moses tells us that Bezalel was called by God to work on designing and building the tabernacle. God equipped him for the task by giving him creative ability through the Spirit of God. But earlier in the chapter, Moses taught the people that, *"All who are gifted among you shall come and make all that the Lord commanded."* Exodus 35:10, NKJV. There were both inherent gifts of creativity and those who God anointed for specific purposes.

We tend to see logic and reasoning as something opposite of creativity. However, during the scientific revolution in the mid 1500's and into the 1600's, many of the leading scientific minds thought logic and reason would scientifically prove that God existed. Our scientific focus is now centered around mankind, not God. Our inherent creative minds and free wills tend to lead us into making assumptions. Therefore, we prove our theories from a faulty place of reasoning.

That is why both naturalists and creationists claim that Isaac Newton is the pioneer of their specific studies. He was one who believed that reason would prove the existence of God. He actually wrote more theological works than he did scientific. However, his scientific methods were instrumental in establishing the sciences we know today. His thoughts were a departure from the traditional Greek way of scientific study and birthed the research and analysist systems in which we are familiar.

https://answersingenesis.org/creation-scientists/misplaced-faith-isaac-newton/

Those who research the way the brain works tell us that our brains visualize patterns better than any modern computer. Our brains have an uncanny ability to connect the dots to what may seem unrelated and bring about solutions and innovations. Scientists call that creativity. We are hard-wired with it. Our brains look for familiar objects in random patterns. Have you ever seen pictures in ink blots? Or faces in clouds? Or trees, sand patterns, or the moon?

This is because we are created in the likeness or image of the Supreme Creative One. We have a choice in how we use our creativity–to build God's Kingdom or our own. But when we remember that it is our Father who instilled this skill set within us, it is easy to give Him the honor and the praise He deserves by using our gifts for His glory.

Practical Application

Have you ever thought about thanking Father for the creative gifts He has given you? Have you asked Him how He would like you to use them? Use this time to write out your praise to Him.

We are all designed to want more. We are explorers by nature. But this quality is best suited when we use it to obtain more understanding of the ways of God and pursue His presence. In all of our reasoning, there comes a point when our words fail. But in that moment, God's words can speak new life and make all things new. What do you need God to recreate in your life? Talk to Him.

FIND ME!

Modern Psalm 8: The Word of God

Jesus answered, "It is written: 'Man shall not live on bread alone, but on every word that comes from the mouth of God"
Matthew 4:4, NIV

The Bible is dusty and sits on a shelf.
My grandmother's favorite she read to herself.

Her devotion was legend in my family tree.
I think it is calling from up there to me.

I open the pages, don't know where to start.
I have a strange tingle from inside my heart.

I read of how David killed a big man
with only a sling and stone in his hand.

Voraciously reading the Bible I see
tales of Noah and Daniel, of Moses and the man from Galilee.

Through tear drops I come to reading the text
"For God so loved..." crying I can't read the rest.

I understand how this book lasts for ages,
when reading the lines there is LIFE in these pages.

My grandmother's Bible is now on display.
The app on my phone brings God's word every day.

Growing up in the heart of the Bible Belt (the South), praying grandmothers and mothers were in no short supply. This was true for both me and the majority of my friends. There is certainly something to be said about the faith of a child. But, often in our teen years, the things of God begin to seem antiquated and too simplistic. We desire adventure and want to explore new ideas. This quality is needed in order to grow, but can be the catalyst that takes us down, what the Bible calls, a crooked path instead of staying in the way that Father has marked out for us.

These praying grandmothers and mothers play an important role in developing our faith. God's word is, *"living and active, sharper than any two-edged sword, piercing to the division of soul and of spirit, of joints and of marrow, and discerning the thoughts and intentions of the heart."* Hebrews 4:12, ESV. When the Word of God is instilled in us as children it lives within the core of our beings and continually calls us back to the path of righteousness.

It is this idea that Paul addresses when he acknowledges to Timothy that he has become a man whom God can use because of what his grandmother and mother instilled in him when he was younger.

> *"I am reminded of your sincere faith, which first dwelt in your grandmother Lois and your mother Eunice, and I am convinced is in you as well. For this reason, I remind you to fan into flame the gift of God, which is in you through the laying on of hands. For God has not given us a spirit of fear, but of power, love, and self-control. So, do not be ashamed of the testimony of our Lord, or of me, His prisoner. Instead join me in suffering for the gospel by the power of God."*
> 2 Timothy 1:5-7, BSB

This idea of what makes for genuine faith has and will continue to be debated throughout the generations. However, by doing a word study, some of the mystery can be uncovered. The word for faith in this scripture is ***pistis***. It means: to be persuaded to trust. It originates with God and is a gift. So, in other words, this kind of faith is something God works within a person in order to persuade or help them believe the truth about His Kingdom. One word study says it this way: The Lord continuously births faith in the yielded believer so they can know what He prefers, i.e., the persuasion of His will (1 Jn 5:4). (HELPS-Word Studies, Strong's 4102; *pistis*.)

Before you take this to mean that you have no responsibility in your faith walk–that it's all God's responsibility–let's look at another scripture. Jesus answered them, *"This is the work of God, that you believe in Him whom He has sent."* John 6:29, ESV. The Greek word used for believe is *pisteuó*. Although it's similar to *pistis*, it means: Having confidence in, or persuading oneself, to trust.

Our faith in God is always a two way street. It's a relationship that's birthed out of God revealing Himself to us, and then in turn, our response back to Him. That's why Paul can say that marriage is a picture of Christ and His Church (His bride). God pursues us through His revealed word and the working of His Spirit; and we respond to Him through submitting to His ways–taking hold of His hand and letting Him lead us on the path that journeys toward our ultimate fulfillment and purpose.

What disconnects us from this relationship? Fear, unbelief, pride, woundedness, unforgiveness, and sin just to name a few. Why? Because those things tempt us to let go of Father's hand in order to self-protect. When we do that, we seek our own path of salvation. However, Jesus is, *"the way, the truth, and the life. No one comes to the Father except through Me."* John 14:6, NKJV. All other roads traveled in a quest for truth and salvation ultimately lead us away from God.

That's why it is so important to learn how to rest in God–to abide in Christ. He continually renews our faith when we seek Him as our ultimate source of life. That seeking requires that we believe His word to be true and we proceed to live by its light. *"Your word is a lamp to my feet and a light to my path."* Psalm 119:105, ESV.

Just like anything else, reading the Bible takes discipline and cultivating a taste for it. It can be difficult to understand at times, but the more we read it, the more understanding Holy Spirit reveals to us. Sometimes, it's hard to swallow because we come across a concept in which our flesh or culture doesn't agree. But the more we learn to submit ourselves to the word of God, the more we become like Jesus and live in the culture of heaven. A great scripture to quote to yourself in learning to walk with God is this one: *"These are the ones I look on with favor: those who are humble and contrite in spirit, and who tremble at my word."* Isaiah 66:2, NIV.

Practical Application

A mature Christian has learned many lessons from familiar Bible stories. Because it's alive, the Word of God is revealed to us in layers of truth. What Bible story speaks to you the most, and why?

Father is always working to draw us close to Himself. Is there something that is tempting you to let go of His hand? Be honest and name it. Then ask Father to hold your hand more tightly and help you overcome.

FIND ME...

Modern Psalm 9: God's Blessing

"The blessing of the Lord enriches, and He adds no sorrow to it."
Proverbs 10:22, BSB

Little faces around the table bring laughter we share,
You have blessed me in so many ways.

The spouse that I love is always right there,
You have blessed me in so many ways.

The purring cat that sits in my lap,
The dog that is there and sits in my chair,
You have blessed me in so many ways.

The list of my friendships are growing so long some might call it a throng,
You have blessed me in so many ways

I help feed the homeless on each Wednesday night,
A hospital visit is my delight,
You have blessed me in so many ways.

I help to send those who move far away
to share the Good News in some other place,
You have blessed me in so many ways.

I've seen other cultures and how You work there,
You have blessed me in so many ways.

To enjoy the beauty in nature I see, mountains and forest, desert and sea,
You have blessed me in so many ways.

This verse could be endless, but I'll move along
and continue the praise in my heart with a song.

"Instruct those who are rich in the present age not to be conceited and not to put their hope in the uncertainty of wealth, but in God, who richly provides all things for us to enjoy. Instruct them to do good, to be rich in good works, and to be generous and ready to share, treasuring up for themselves a firm foundation for the future, so that they may take hold of that which is truly life." 1 Timothy 6: 17-19, BSB.

Have you ever heard the phrase, "Blessed to be a blessing?" This idea is found in the very first book of the Bible–Genesis. However, we see this principle in both the Old and New Testaments. It is certainly a teaching Paul stressed in his letters to the churches he fathered.

He said this to the Corinthian church: *"Now He who supplies seed to the sower and bread for food will supply and multiply your store of seed and will increase the harvest of your righteousness. You will be enriched in every way to be generous on every occasion, so that through us your giving will produce thanksgiving to God. For this ministry of service is not only supplying the needs of the saints but is also overflowing in many expressions of thanksgiving to God."* 2 Corinthians 9:10-12, BSB

Paul addressed the church in Philippi in this manner: *"And as you Philippians know, in the early days of the gospel, when I left Macedonia, no church but you partnered with me in the matter of giving and receiving. For even while I was in Thessalonica, you provided for my needs again and again. Not that I am seeking a gift, but I am looking for the fruit that may be credited to your account."* Philippians 4:15-17, BSB

This was sound Apostolic advice from their spiritual father. It mimicked the call Abraham received as the father of many nations. This is the story in which we get the phrase, "Blessed to be a blessing."

> *"Now the Lord said to Abram, 'Go from your country and your kindred and your father's house to the land that I will show you. And I will make of you a great nation, and I will bless you and make your name great, so that you will be a blessing. I will bless those who bless you, and him who dishonors you I will curse, and in you all the families of the earth shall be blessed."*
> *Genesis 12:1-3, ESV*

When God told Abraham that he would be a blessing, the Hebrew word used there is **berakah**. It means a gift, a present, a source of prosperity and peace. God chose Abraham in order that He might form a people who would bless the whole world. This idea of being chosen or elected in a Biblical sense is never so that the one chosen is seen as having something others do not, but rather for the sake of God's mission to reconcile the world back to Himself. The twelve tribes that formed the nation of Israel were Abraham's descendants. Israel had a specific call, to make the salvation of the Lord known throughout the whole world. *"In your seed all the nations of the earth shall be blessed, because you have obeyed My voice."* Genesis 22:18, NKJV. The blessing is such that all of mankind might be brought into the Kingdom; bought back from the consequences of sin; and live in the light of the Lord's face.

The beautiful thing about the New Covenant (the age in which we live), is that each of us who have a relationship with Jesus are elected and chosen to be a blessing. We are to seek out ways of extending the kindness of God so that others might come to know Him. By sharing the blessings given to us, it is a witness that God truly is our source of provision and that we are grateful to be the benefactors of His many blessings. It allows us to express the love of God in tangible ways.

You cannot outgive God. Every time you give out of gratitude, God gives back to you in return. You may see it immediately, or it may be stored up for you in heaven's storehouses; but make no mistake–it's there. Just like anything in the Kingdom, giving will cause you to evaluate the condition of your heart. If we give out of gratitude and because we know that we are blessed to be a blessing, then our giving is done in faith. If we give simply to get, then we need to mature in our understanding of this principle–and check our motives. There are rich treasures stored up in heaven for the purpose of advancing God's Kingdom. We can draw on those deposits through prayer. But we must be people who have become cheerful in our giving in order to do so. The attitude in which we give is key.

Practical Application

What are some ways you can give of yourself, your time, or your finances?

What is your greatest fear when it comes to the giving of these things? Ask Father to help you see the root of that fear and to give you opportunities this week to overcome through giving.

Hi!

find me...

Always take time to stop and appreciate the things God has provided...
—Jonah 4

Modern Psalm 10: Our Father

"As a father shows compassion to his children, so the Lord shows compassion to those who fear Him."
Psalms 103:13, ESV

I sit at the beach
And look at the waves,
And see people walking beside the bay.

Just over there a surfer or two,
And kids building sandcastles
More than a few.

I feel really special while sitting here sunnin'
And see my own children
Come by just a runnin'.

I daydream how ABBA must feel looking down
At all His kids laughing
And playing around.

I realize I'm singing and giving You praise,
At first just a mumble
Then both hands are raised…

To honor You Father
For all that You do.
My praises continue…

…now where are those shoes?

It is not a secret that our culture seems to devalue the role of father. Often, fathers are portrayed in the media as inept and insignificant when it comes to relating to their wives and children. And yet, the role of a father is the cornerstone of the way God designed family. They are not just the other adult attempting to parent. Fathers are designed to have a different parenting style than their female counterpart. When each work together, they bring health and vitality to the home.

That rough-housing that fathers tend to provide when playing with their children encourages healthy emotional growth and risk taking. Fathers also tend to be more justice oriented which instills a deep sense of right and wrong in the character of their children. And they lean toward seeing their children in relation to the rest of the world. Mothers tend to create their world around their children. When both are in play, you have a child who learns they have a place of belonging and yet a responsibility to the larger community.

Focus on the Family, "The Significance of a Father's Influence," https://www.focusonthefamily.com/family-qa/the-significance-of-a-fathers-influence/

1 John 3:1, NIV reads, *"See what great love the Father has lavished on us, that we should be called children of God! And that is what we are! The reason the world does not know us is that it did not know Him."* This scripture is troubling for many. Not because they disagree with it so much, but because it is difficult to imagine God in this way. This happens most often when we feel as though our relationship with our earthly father was distant or hurtful.

> *"The he (Absalom) said to his servants, 'Look, Joab's field is next to mine, and he has barley there. Go and set it on fire.' So, Absalom's servants set the field on fire. Then Joab did go to Absalom's house, and he said to him, 'Why have your servants set my field on fire?' Absalom said to Joab, 'Look, I sent word to you and said, 'Come here so I can send you to the king to ask, 'Why have I come from Geshur? It would be better for me if I were still there!' Now then, I want to see the king's face, and if I am guilty of anything, let him put me to death.'"*
> *2 Samuel 14:30-32, NIV*

Many wonderful things can be said about King David but being a great father may not make the list. He certainly prepared Solomon for the task of building the temple, but when it came to his other children, they often rebelled against him and acted in a manner that dishonored God. Of course, royal life was different and the heir to the throne received the most attention from the king. But you can see in this statement from Absalom what he needed most from his father. We are told he wanted to see the king's face.

Absalom had tried to dethrone his father and had been banished. In an effort toward resolution, David had allowed Absalom back into Jerusalem, but would not allow his son back into his presence. This is what is meant by "seeing his face." This rejection of Absalom on an ongoing basis was more than the young prince could handle. He ended up going to great lengths to get his father to acknowledge him as his son once again. Although Absalom's character was certainly not trustworthy, we see the pain in his heart that likely drove some of his poor choices–the pain of a boy who needed his father's approval.

Psalm 105:4, NIV tells us, *"Look to the Lord and His strength; seek His face always."* What does it mean to seek God's face? It means to spend time in His presence. We do that through a relationship with Him that is made tangible through the Holy Spirit. This is what Jesus came to do–to reconcile us back to the Father. Our sin separates us, but through Jesus we are made righteous so that we might boldly enter the throne of grace. (Hebrews 4:16).

Then, when we seek God's face, we get to know Him. We become like Him. We find that we are not spiritual orphans, but highly valued children in the Kingdom. Our hearts are put to rest in His presence, and we are strengthened to become who we were originally created to be because we experience the love of our Heavenly Father. We find He is what we have needed all along. He is our true sense of belonging.

Luke 12:32, ESV says this, *"Fear not, little flock, for it is your Father's good pleasure to give you the kingdom."* That means He will not withhold from you that which is needed to become the mature sons and daughters He seeks. He delights in His children and wants to see each of us fulfill our purpose and experience the fullness of His love. He cares for us with a love that casts out all fear of rejection. And His greatest joy is watching His children reach their full potential in Him.

Practical Application

Look up Proverbs 3:11-12. Why does Father bring discipline to us and what are the benefits?

Earthly fathers are imperfect people who most likely did the best they knew how by their children. Ask your heavenly Father to reveal His heart toward you–His child. If there are areas of unresolved pain relating to your earthly dad, ask Father to fill those places with His love and protection.

FIND ME!

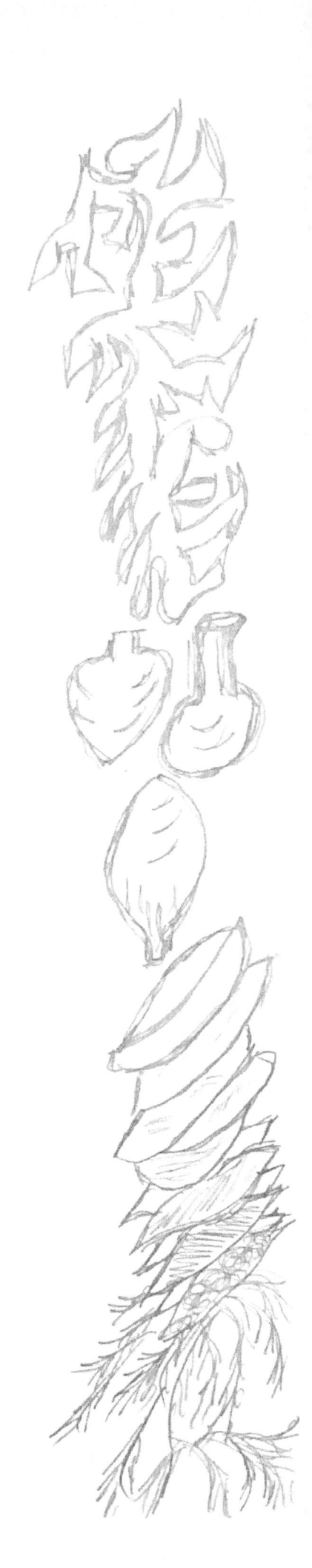

Modern Psalm 11: Dividing Walls

"Let the peace of Christ rule in your hearts, for this you were called as members of one body. And be thankful."
Colossians 3:15, BSB

They all look alike. They all act like this!
I hear people shouting and shaking raised fists.

Anger spawns hatred, fear and mistrust.
Lines drawn as in battle, conflict a must.

My spirit is saddened. I see the display,
"Injustice" is broadcast on media waves.

I know You're not happy when you look at us.
But God You are sovereign. Your precepts are just.

Your Spirit is moving on some in the crowd.
To advance Your Kingdom and debase the proud.

Satan stirs trouble to grab our attention.
But he is defeated when mercy's extended.

We each have a place created for You,
Your Spirit fits perfect and changes our view.

The struggle continues between wrong and right,
Your Spirit gives guidance and brings us to life.

Advancing Your Kingdom remains our life's passion.
We grow toward Jesus, a noble reaction.

National unrest. I have heard many people say they have never seen division in America like it is being displayed today. I believe that to be true for most generations. However, our Founding Fathers came to this land in search of freedom from tyranny. Most fled the religious persecution that plagued Europe. We also have learned in our history classes that as America grew, her national identity of freedom for all men needed to be addressed. The issue of slavery divided us. We saw civil war between the northern states and the southern states. We again saw a surge of civil unrest in the 1960's as young people addressed social injustices. But I have to agree that the hostility which has surfaced in our nation today does seem unprecedented in its fierceness.

Ephesians 2:1-2, NIV states, *"As for you, you were dead in your transgressions and sins, in which you used to live when you followed the ways of this world and of the ruler of the kingdom of the air, the spirit who is now at work in those who are disobedient."* The truth is the world system, that is dominated by "the prince of the air," will always be full of unrest. Satan (the one called the prince of the air) is masterful at creating an "us against them" mentality. Certainly, injustices need to be addressed in the world. But if the goal is for one group to have unrighteous power over another, to seek revenge through violent means, or to bring about chaos and anarchy, then we can be certain that there is a demonic assignment taking place designed to kill, steal, and destroy that which God deems as good and right in His eyes.

Being prejudice toward others is not something that is new. It is as old as time. It is a result of sin entering the world. The Apostle Paul had much to say when it came to our tendency toward being prejudice toward others.

> *"For there are many rebellious people, full of meaningless talk and deception, especially those of the circumcision group. They must be silenced, because they are disrupting whole households by teaching things they ought not to teach–and that for the sake of dishonest gain. One of Crete's own prophets has said it: "Cretans are always liars, evil brutes, lazy gluttons."*
> *Titus 1:10-12, NIV*

If taken out of context, it can seem that Paul himself was demeaning in his statement about Cretans. But that is far from the truth. This letter was written to

Paul's disciple Titus who had been placed over the church in Crete. Paul was giving instructions on how to bring order within the church due to opposing mindsets. The statement Paul made about Cretans was a quote that was said about their people by a leader of their people. He used something that was familiar to the culture to make a comparison to the present situation. He instructed Titus to teach sound doctrine (Titus 2) and to understand that he would have to deal with the ones who were adamant about bringing division– namely those who wanted to enforce the Old Covenant laws. By making the statement about the character of Cretans, he was saying it's in the Jewish believer's mindset to demand that everyone follow Jewish customs. But then he goes on to give Titus a strategy in order to subdue conflict.

In Acts 10:34-35, ESV, Peter says, *"...I truly understand that God shows no partiality, but in every nation anyone who fears Him and does what is right is acceptable to Him."* That is the beautiful thing about God's Kingdom. All people, no matter their class, color, education, social status, or upbringing can enter into the family of God. Once brought into the Kingdom, we then find a new culture to learn that allows for all people to be united and joined together. The dividing walls of hostility which Satan loves to use are eradicated and we learn the ways of love, honor, acceptance, and belonging.

Continuing his lesson concerning the divisive "prince of the air," Paul says to the Ephesians, *"For He Himself (Jesus) is our peace who has made the two groups one and has destroyed the barrier, the dividing wall of hostility, by setting aside in His flesh the law with its commands and regulations. His purpose was to create in Himself one new humanity out of the two, thus making peace, and in one body to reconcile both of them to God through the cross, by which He put to death their hostility."* Ephesians 2:14-16, NIV

That is the crux of the Gospel. The cross is the Great Equalizer for all of mankind. We were all sons of disobedience, separated from the love of the Father. However, once we are born again, we find the acceptance and belonging we all need. We then seek to bring others into that same relationship as we learn to honor one another–maturing in the ways of God's Kingdom.

The pages of every history book you have ever studied are filled with nations rising up against nations. Certainly, we have a responsibility to do good to the world in which we now live. But just remember, when you are tempted to be overwhelmed by all the unrest and rumors of violence and hostility, know that Jesus has made you co-heir with Him in His unshakable Kingdom.

Practical Application

God's plan is for all men everywhere to come to Him. Look up Acts 2:17-18. Peter is quoting the prophet Joel and explaining that what Joel said would come to pass was now here. What would it look like in our day if we were to realize that we can be united through the power of the Holy Spirit?

Be honest with yourself. Are you prejudice toward a certain group of people due to their skin color, their political affiliation, or their cultural differences? You don't have to be in complete agreement with someone in order to show them respect and honor. In your prayer time today, ask Father to show you your own prejudices and what He would have you do about it.

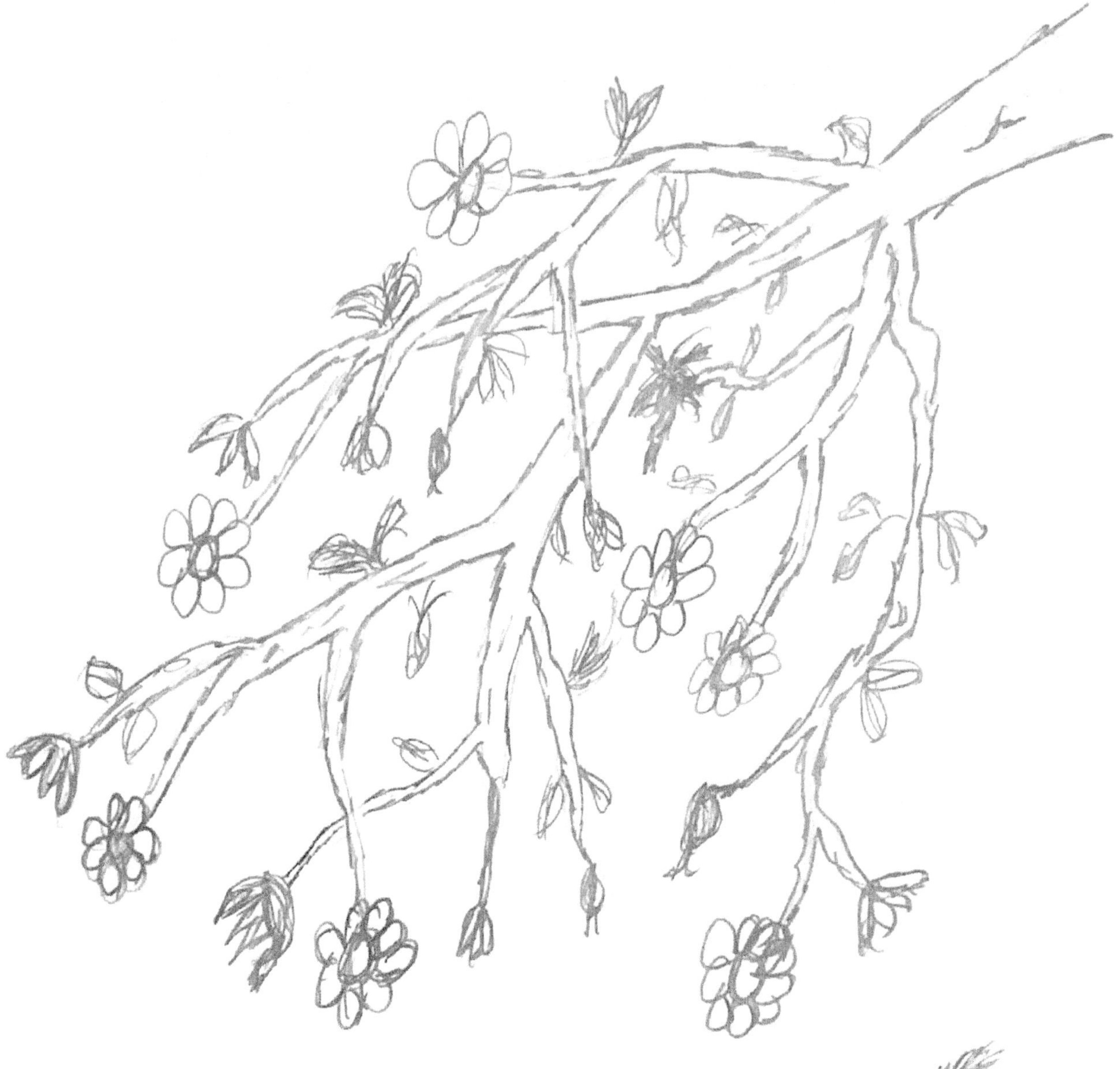

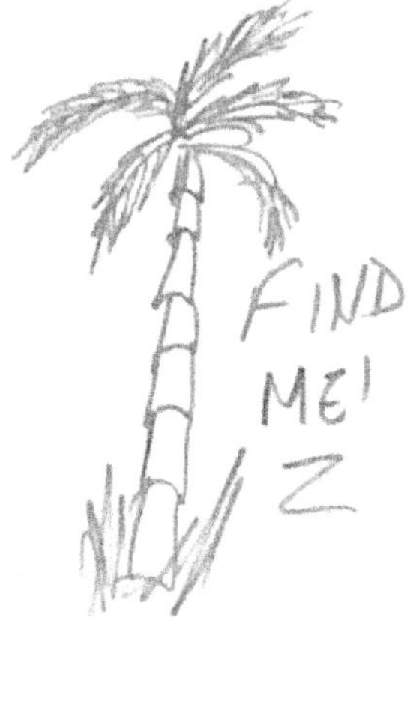
FIND
ME!
Z

Modern Psalm 12: Growing Together

"So then, just as you received Christ Jesus as Lord, continue to live your lives in Him, rooted and built up in Him, strengthened in the faith as you were taught, and overflowing with thankfulness."
Colossians 2:6-7, NIV

*I love watching springtime bud into life
leaving the winter behind with its blight.*

*Time to raise young ones, time to prepare
future generations, to pass on the heir.*

*I think how our Father helps us to grow
by passing on knowledge we each one should know.*

*We learn from the Bible, we learn from His kids,
we learn from the pastors; His Spirit He sends.*

*I'm so very thankful as I see the growth
of those in His Kingdom, it strengthens my soul.*

The short answer, according to NASA, on why we have seasons is: Earth's tilted axis causes them. Throughout the year, different parts of Earth receive the sun's most direct rays. So, when the North Pole tilts toward the Sun, it's summer in the Northern Hemisphere. And when the South Pole tilts toward the sun, it's winter in the Northern Hemisphere.

https://spaceplace.nasa.gov/seasons/en/

Most of us, apart from the allergies associated with it, love the new growth that spring brings. This is especially true after the cold, dreary, drawn-out days of winter. Father often teaches us Biblical principles through the way He designed creation. In the same manner which the earth embraces seasonal change, we grow spiritually as well. As believers, we walk through seasons in our personal growth that mimic all four natural seasons. Fall brings with it a sense of change and the need to get prepared for what lies ahead. Winter can seem like a season where things that were once vibrant begin to fade. Death takes place: death of a dream; death of past ministry or occupation; death of our fleshly ways. Of course, in Christ, the only things that perish are that which have no eternal value. Once we walk through this process, we enter spring. There is a renewed sense of hope. Purpose seems to be restored or refashioned. New opportunities are revealed that allows for the growth that has taken place within us. This then leads to summer where everything seems bright and cheery–as though nothing is standing in the way of us fulfilling our new assignment or going beyond where we were in previous seasons.

> *"For everything there is a season, and a time for every matter under heaven: a time to be born, and a time to die; a time to plant, and a time to pluck up what is planted; a time to kill, and a time to heal; a time to break down, and a time to build up; a time to weep, and a time to laugh; a time to mourn, and a time to dance; a time to cast away stones, and a time to gather stones together; a time to embrace, and a time to refrain from embracing; a time to seek, an a time to lose; a time to keep, and a time to cast away; a time to tear, and a time to sew; a time to keep silent, and a time to speak; a time to love, and a time to hate; a time for war, and a time for peace."*
> *Ecclesiastes 3:1-8, ESV*

Change is inevitable. The question is not, "Will I experience change?" The right question is, "Who will help me when I experience change?" Of course, the first place we need to look when change occurs is the heart of our Father. He says in His word, *"He will never leave you, nor forsake you."* Deuteronomy 31:6, NIV

For us in the Church age, part of that promise is that we have been placed in the family of God. In that, we have been given spiritual parents (mentors) who can help us walk through the seasons of life we are certain to face. Although hurt people truly do hurt people–healed people look for ways to help others heal. A good mentor is someone who is aware of their own frailties and shortcomings. They have learned how to take the lessons from their past mistakes and use them as guideposts for others. They spend time working on themselves through prayer, being mentored, and putting the Word of God into practice. They are always looking for revealed nuggets of God's character to share with others. They glean from the wisdom being imparted about Father's heart and ways. They are constantly growing and pull others into the process by cultivating an atmosphere that is relational and growth-minded.

When we entered into a relationship with Jesus, it was just the beginning. We now are on a journey to become like Him. In order to do that, we are in constant change–letting go of our ways and taking on His. Finding a mentor who will help us when things get difficult, or share in our joys, shows that we are serious about our walk with Christ. It's not weakness. It's wisdom. We all have areas of weakness where we need the help of those who know how to overcome.

The image below is a helpful tool when assessing where you are and what needs to change on a practical level. If we are going to make it through our winter seasons back into spring, it requires purposeful growth.

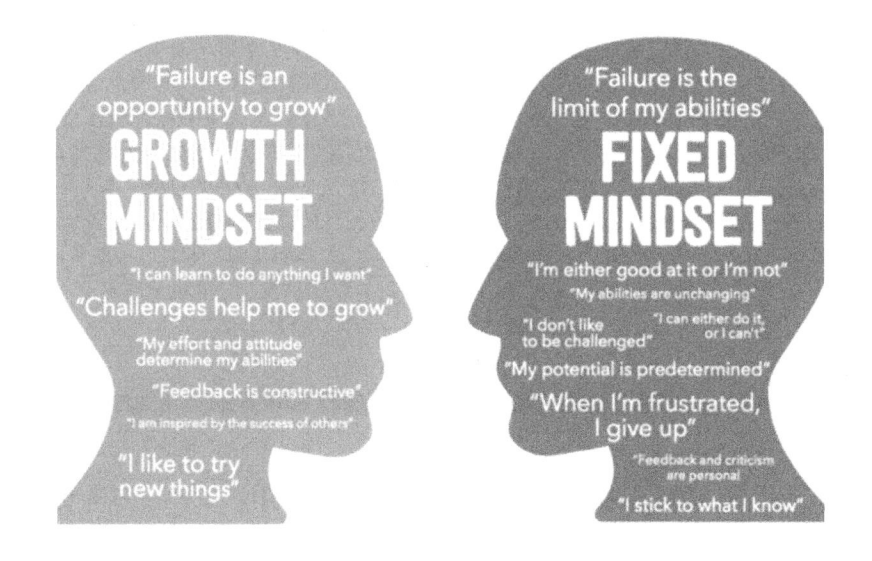

GROWTH MINDSET
- "Failure is an opportunity to grow"
- "I can learn to do anything I want"
- "Challenges help me to grow"
- "My effort and attitude determine my abilities"
- "Feedback is constructive"
- "I am inspired by the success of others"
- "I like to try new things"

FIXED MINDSET
- "Failure is the limit of my abilities"
- "I'm either good at it or I'm not"
- "My abilities are unchanging"
- "I don't like to be challenged"
- "I can either do it, or I can't"
- "My potential is predetermined"
- "When I'm frustrated, I give up"
- "Feedback and criticism are personal"
- "I stick to what I know"

Practical Application

Look up Prov 22:6, Mark 16:15, and Acts 14:21. Why is important to be mentored and then learn to mentor others?

Look up Colossians 1:10 and 2 Peter 3:18. What spiritual season are you walking through? Identify what needs to change in you while in this season and then ask God to show you who might help you in the process.

FIND!
ME

Modern Psalm 13: Cleansing

"For by one Spirit we were all baptized into one body,
whether Jews or Greeks, whether slaves or free,
and we were all made to drink of one Spirit."
1 Corinthians 12:13, NKJV

A trickle of water along the ground,
a trickle of water—how profound!

Substance much needed to continue life,
Harbors no guilt bears no strife.

Yet God has given us water you see,
To keep us alive, much like the trees.

And much like the water, His spirit gives life,
Watered dry places soon will revive.

Bearing the fruit, we all grow to share,
Love, joy, and peace with bountiful flair.

"Water was the center of life in many ancient cultures. In Greek mythology, one of the most ancient and powerful gods was Neptune, the god of the sea. Ancient Greek literature, such as The Odyssey by Homer (about 800 B.C.E.), mentions sea monsters, whirlpools, and harrowing voyages upon the sea. In India, the Ganges River was considered sacred from historical accounts over 3000 years old. To the ancient Egyptians, the Nile River was the political, economic, and life-sustaining center of their kingdom. Without the Nile, Egypt would be as barren as its nearby deserts. Ancient civilizations' respect for water grew from their absolute need of it. Like today, water sustained life in many ways."

http://what-when-how.com/water-science/water-and-cultures-in-the-ancient-world/

The word water appears 582 times in the Old Testament. It is used to describe creation and destruction, purification, regeneration, revival, and love. Water is also a metaphor for the Holy Spirit. Just as ancient civilizations were dependent on a vast resource of water in order to thrive, Christians also need the refreshing outpour of the Holy Spirit to enliven our walk with Christ. The Prophet Ezekiel had a vision involving water that came at a time when Israel's collective faith seemed dry and barren. God pulled the curtain back on the activities within the temple and revealed to His Prophet the corruption and sinful behavior that was taking place. His priests were guilty, and apathy had gripped the heart of the nation at large.

> *"Then he brought me back to the door of the temple, and behold, water was issuing from below the threshold of the temple toward the east (for the temple faced east) ...Going on eastward with a measuring line in his hand, the man measured a thousand cubits, and then led me through the water, and it was ankle-deep. Again, he measured a thousand, and led me through the water, and it was knee-deep. Again, he measured a thousand and led me through the water, and it was waist-deep. Again, he measured a thousand, and it was a river that I could not pass through, for the water had risen. It was deep enough to swim in, a river that could not be passed through.*
> *Ezekiel 47:1-6, ESV*

The direction the water flowed indicated that the water came from where the seven golden lampstands were situated within the temple. The candlesticks represented the presence of the Lord. The debate on whether Ezekiel is picturing the literal temple being filled with water, or the heavenly temple that the earthly one is modeled after, is ongoing among Bible scholars. However, we can be sure that the water represents the presence of the Holy Spirit and the subsequent blessing that He brings. He is able to completely cleanse every stain and make us ready to be the people God has called us to be. This is the truth of the Gospel message–no one is clean in the eyes of the Lord. We have all *"fallen short of the glory of God."* Romans 3:23. But because Jesus took our sin upon Himself at the cross and shed His blood in our place, we now can be presented before a holy God as righteous and clean.

Notice Ezekiel's vision of water began as a trickle and ended in a flood. Mankind, animals, plants, and insects all rely on water as a source of life. Natural water on dry ground stimulates growth. Living water on a dry heart also brings life. It sets in motion the purpose for our lives that we were designed to fulfill from the very beginning. Life brings growth. Growth brings fruit. Fruit brings glory to God.

God's purpose for us is to spend time with Him, bear spiritual fruit, and to share that fruit with others. You may feel as though you are not clean enough to worship God freely and to be accepted by Him. If you have sin in your heart, please know that through confession and repentance, God will cleanse every ounce of what separates you from His presence. Just be honest about it and ask the Holy Spirit to work deep within your soul. Tell Him that you want to bring Him glory more than you want to hold onto the thing that brings pain to your heart.

God is a healer. He is a redeemer. He is a savior. There is nothing too hard for Him. As a matter of fact, Ezekiel's vision of the river flowing through the temple ends with this beautiful word picture of true healing and redemption. *"And on the banks, on both sides of the river, there will grow all kinds of trees for food. Their leaves will not wither, nor their fruit fail, but they will bear fresh fruit every month, because the water for them flows from the sanctuary. Their fruit will be for food, and their leaves for healing."* Ezekiel 47:12, ESV

God Himself is building a civilization, a people. He does that by unifying us through the cleansing power of the blood of Christ and the outpouring of His Spirit. And God is no respecter of persons. All who believe may enter His eternal city.

Practical Application

Look up Acts 1:5. Do you have a relationship with the Holy Spirit? Have you been baptized in the Spirit? Like any relationship, you must cultivate God's presence. Write out what you believe is holding you back in any way from receiving in this manner.

Look up John 4:10. Jesus says all you need to do is ask and He will give you living water. Ask Jesus to refresh you with the presence of the Holy Spirit. Write out your "Yes" to Him.

find me!

Modern Psalm 14: Child-like Faith

"But Jesus said, 'Let the little children come to me and do not hinder them, for to such belongs the Kingdom of Heaven.'"
Matthew 19:14, ESV

Little hands hold to mine
And little eyes, how they shine.
Having no fear or doubt of anything.

They only dream of happy things.
Their laughter floats on angel's wings.

And in their mouth the Lord perfects praise.
Lord help me come to you as a little child

You know how we could right our wrongs.
Spend some time with Him alone,
and let His waters flow into our soul.

Then lift our hearts to Him in praise
and thank the Lord every day.

And in our mouth the Lord perfects praise.
Lord help me come to You as a little child.

The words to this poem were penned as lyrics to a song when our son was old enough to see me from his baby carrier and reach for my fingers. Our older daughter was about three years of age. She was playful, loved to laugh, always believing, and full of trust. I still remember to this day, the picture that was portrayed to me in that moment. My children trusted me to take care of them. And truly, no matter how old we get, or mature we believe ourselves to be, this is still the way to present ourselves before our heavenly Father–as His faith-filled child.

> *"At that time the disciples came to Jesus and asked, 'Who then, is the greatest in the Kingdom of Heaven? He called a little child to Him and placed the child among them. And He said: 'Truly I tell you, unless you change and become like little children, you will never enter the Kingdom of Heaven. Therefore, whoever takes the lowly position of this child is the greatest in the Kingdom of Heaven. And whoever welcomes one such child in My name, welcomes Me."*
> Matthew 18:1-5, NIV

The disciples had grown up in Greco-Roman society where importance was put upon obtaining stature and position. Their question was a byproduct of their culture. But Kingdom culture is radically different from the world's standards of achievement and status. Jesus tells His disciples that their way of life would need to radically change if they were to enter the Kingdom at all. Then He sits a child upon His knee and begins to teach.

Jesus compares the character needed to enter the Kingdom of heaven to a child. According to commentary by William Barclay, a child exhibits these three things: humility, dependence, and trust.

https://www.studylight.org/commentaries/dsb/matthew-18.html

True humility doesn't devalue self. It displays the value of all people. Jesus showed us true humility when He *"being found in appearance as a man, He humbled Himself..."* Philippians 2:8, NIV. Humility serves others. It doesn't ambitiously run others over or maneuver them out of the way in order to get something.

Children are naturally dependent upon the care of their parents. Until they get older, it doesn't occur to them to strike out on their own. They are perfectly content with needing others to care for them. It is this quality that we need to cultivate with our heavenly Father. He cares for us, and we need His care. The more dependent we are on the attentive love of God, the more we grow into mature sons and daughters.

Children, who are cared for, never worry about running out of food. They trust that their parents will meet their needs. Because of that, they go about their day playing and doing things that delight their soul. It is this kind of trust that Jesus told His disciples they needed in order to be great in heaven.

Barclay goes on to say, "The child's humility is the pattern of the Christian's behavior to his fellow men, and the child's dependence and trust are the pattern of the Christian's attitude towards God, the Father of all."

Our growth in the things of God is directly related to our dependance upon Him. Our faith can either be childish or child-like–there is a difference. Childish faith will make demands of God to answer its own willful requests. It wants its way and gets angry when God doesn't bend to its pleas. Child-like faith rests in the care of Father and humbly looks for ways to serve others. It's not consumed with its own gain.

When Jesus cleansed the temple, Matthew tells us two things occurred. First, He overturned the tables where they sold animals for the offering, and where they converted money from other nations to pay the temple tax. Then, He healed the blind and lame. (Matthew 21). The Pharisees and Scribes were angry. Mathew says this, *"But when the chief priests and the teachers of the law saw the wonderful things he did and the children shouting in the temple courts, 'Hosanna to the Son of David,' they were indignant. 'Do you hear what these children are saying?' they asked him. 'Yes,' replied Jesus, 'have you never read, "From the lips of children and infants you, Lord, have called forth your praise?"'* (Matthew 21:15-16, NIV).

The word used for called forth is **katartizó**. It means restored, ordained, prepared, or put to its proper use. What was being called forth? –praise for the miracles and wonders that Jesus did. Who were calling forth, or as some translations say, perfecting praise? –children. They didn't question who He was. They simply rejoiced in Him. However, the "important" teachers and leaders of Israel, had lost their child-like wonderment in God and His promises.

Practical Application

Many times, God told the children of Israel if they would obey Him, He would bless them. Jesus said, *"If anyone loves Me, he will keep my word."* John 14:23, NKJV. Where do you have difficulty in obedience to the Father?

When we hear the word obedience, we often think of a list that starts with the words "Do not do (fill in the blank)." However, when we approach Father with child-like faith, we find that He wants us to live in the presence of the Holy Spirit. If we keep reading in John, we find that one of the gifts Holy Spirit gives us is peace. What would peace look like in those areas of disobedience you identified?

FIND
ME...

Modern Psalm 15: Rest

"…He leads me beside still waters. He restores my soul."
Psalm 23:2-3, ESV

The stress I feel is so severe
To feel some respite, I draw near the waterfall.
A mere trickle from a brook,
I venture here to take a look at the waterfall.

Maybe 30 meters high,
Much too high for me to scale,
to see the brook above is quite a trail.
The climate is just sweltering
On the journey I was melting.

I dream of cowboys herding steers and
schooner drivers stopping here to rest in the shade.
I cool my feet to calm the mood, lately it seems I only brood.
But seeing water coursing down begins to calm the ebbing frown.

The waterfall's a steady stream,
I think I hear it calling me to embrace the flow.
I stumble, slide, and mostly slip to the fount,
I must admit I had not intended to go.

Water cool, arms held wide, face turned upwards,
I just cried at the release. Genuine release.

You My Father will provide
the resting place we must not deride to be with you.

I left that day with new perspective
A daily encounter is my directive
to spend more time with You.

Thank you God for leading me to the waterfall.

Stress is a natural part of our lives. When we say, 'I'm stressed," we are noticing our physical body in a heightened state of readiness. Our stress response happens when we perceive danger and is a way of strengthening our muscles and alertness in order to respond quickly. How we react to perceived threats determines the degree of the stress response in our body. This natural response should help us see clearer and react appropriately so that we can avoid danger.

But sometimes that stress level is increased exponentially, to the point where we just can't see past the circumstances. They seem too high to climb, too far to go around, and the intensity of the heat brings our faculties to the boiling point. This happens when we are under chronic stress. Desperate for relief, we look for a place of solitude to escape if only for a moment. We allow our minds to wander to places more peaceful in an attempt to enjoy at least a strained state of relaxation.

In general, the constant sound of water is soothing–waves lapping onto the beach, the bubbling of a stream, or water coursing from a waterfall no matter how high the drop. The air near a waterfall seems cooler, and often a mist is present if the drop is high enough. Sounds echo against the sides of the opposing banks creating a sense of closeness with nature. Our minds tend to wander to an enjoyable activity concerning water–swimming, camping, fishing, hiking–something more soothing than our present state of affairs.

David knew this to be true. He used this same analogy of water as he wrote his most famous Psalm.

> *"The Lord is my shepherd; I shall not want. He makes me lie down in green pastures. He leads me beside still waters. He restores my soul. He leads me in paths of righteousness for his name's sake. Even though I walk through the valley of the shadow of death, I will fear no evil, for you are with me; your rod and your staff, they comfort me. You prepare a table before me in the presence of my enemies; you anoint my head with oil; my cup overflows. Surely goodness and mercy shall follow me all the days of my life, and I shall dwell in the house of the Lord forever.*
> *Psalm 23, ESV*

Father knows that we will face certain trouble in this life; and He has a place for us to release anxiety. Acts 1:5, NIV states, *"For John baptized with water, but in a few days you will be baptized with the Holy Spirit."* When we immerse ourselves in the presence of Holy Spirit, we feel the tangible peace of God that surpasses all understanding. (Phil 4:6-9) It is in this fellowship with God where our overwhelming anxieties are brought to genuine release.

Father gives us His peace in any circumstance. The busyness may not end, the circumstance may still be there, but God's peace will override the stress that tells us the result of our particular problem will be our undoing.

But here's the thing, we often live in chronic stress because we don't understand that the issues we face in this life are designed to help us surrender to God in deeper ways. Even as believers, we reject God's comfort and think we have to figure out our own means of escape. We fail to realize, that the more we rest in the presence of Holy Spirit, the more our prayers are answered. The more we give our anxious thoughts to God, the more aware we are of the table He prepares for us in the midst of whatever we perceive as an enemy.

Jesus said this, *"Come to me, all who labor and are heavy laden, and I will give you rest."* Matthew 11:28 ESV.

- The Greek word used for labor is **kapiao**. It means growing weary or, working with effort either physically or mentally.
- The Greek word used for heavy laden is **phortizo.** It means overloaded or weighted down.
- The Greek word used for rest is **anapauo.** It is a verb meaning to make rest; or take ease; to give intermission to one's labor.

Once we are in Christ, we truly do make the choice whether to live in chronic stress or to appropriate the peace of God through the rest that Christ gives. We can walk in true Spirit-filled rest, that intermission from our weariness and over-burdened efforts of rescuing ourselves from trouble, or we can continue to carry our heavy load ourselves. One is part of our inheritance as children of God. The other is our inheritance from our sinful nature. There is no condemnation in the process of learning to give these things over–but let's make sure that we meet God at the refreshing streams He provides for us. His watering holes have the clearest, coolest, most sparkling blue water that any of us have ever seen.

Practical Application

Look up Isaiah 44:3. Identify an area of your life that is thirsty for God's water: finances, relationship issues, school assignments, etc. Write out your need in that area and spend time asking God to bring you to a place of rest.

Look up Psalm 63:1. Think about the times you have been saturated in God's presence. Remind yourself of what that was like by writing it down. Ask God for a fresh infilling of His Spirit and then expect Him to answer that prayer.

FIND ME!
JONAH 4

SMILES ARE CONTAGIOUS

Modern Psalm 16: Morning Prayer

"In the morning, LORD, you hear my voice; in the morning I lay my requests before You and wait expectantly."
Psalms 5:3, NIV

20 more minutes to sleep. 20 more to rest.
I clinch my eyes and try to rest
But there is a stirring deep in my chest
To give You Lord the first and best.

Each day Your mercies begin anew.
They drench our lives much as the dew
Waters the earth and the plants,
Calming our fears and the rants
we selfishly share with our peers.

Your mercies cover our human mistakes
and draw us to that place of peace we each crave.
Thank You Father each day is new.
Thank You Lord for the dew.

Are you one of those perky morning people? Maybe you truly are, but most people say they love to hit that snooze button a few times before they attempt to get out of bed. Our sleep patterns, like most things in our lives, are products of our habits. Sleep studies suggest that most American's do not get adequate rest. We burn the candles at both ends and wonder why we can't seem to fall asleep when we are chronically tired, but truthfully, we have trained our body to react to our demands. Once the cycle is on repeat enough, it just becomes our norm. A web article in Healthline says: "Difficulty getting up in the morning isn't just about loving your sleep and hating mornings. Lifestyle factors, medical conditions, and medications can make it hard to wake up. These include:

- parasomnias, such as sleepwalking, sleep talking, and night terrors
- sleep apnea, which causes periods of stopped breathing during sleep
- sleep deficiency, which can involve not getting good quality sleep, or sleep deprivation, which is not getting enough sleep
- stress and anxiety, which can interfere with your ability to fall asleep or stay asleep
- depression, which has been linked to excessive daytime sleepiness and insomnia
- circadian rhythm sleep disorders, which can prevent you from developing a regular sleep routine, such as shift work sleep disorder and irregular sleep-wake disorder
- certain medications, including beta blockers, certain muscle relaxants, and selective serotonin reuptake inhibitor antidepressants
- chronic pain, which can make it difficult to get a good night's sleep"

https://www.healthline.com/health/cant-wake-up#causes

These same sleep experts will also tell you that an enjoyable morning routine helps you to set the day's expectations and put in place the needed structure in order to maintain proper sleep patterns.

> *"Give ear to my words, O LORD, Consider my meditation. Give heed to the voice of my cry, My King and my God. For to you, I will pray. My voice You shall hear in the morning, O LORD; In the morning I will direct it to You, And I will look up"*
> *Psalm 5:1-3, ESV*

David was a man who consistently met with God in the mornings through prayer. He is known as the greatest king in Israel's history. He is also known as a man after God's own heart. How did he learn what God's heart was like? Most likely through prayer.

The dawn of a new day brings God's mercies into view. *"Because of the Lord's great love, we are not consumed, for His compassions never fail. They are new every morning; great is Your faithfulness."* Lamentations 3:22-23, NIV. When I set my intention to meet with God first thing in the morning, He is faithful to meet with me. His presence at the beginning of my day sets the tone for how I cope with the circumstances thrown my way. However, if I fail to rise and spend that time with Father, I tend to notice snarky replies and attitudes creeping into my daily dealings with people–maybe even outright abrasive conversations. Because He is merciful, a continual conversation with Him throughout the day will correct my attitude, but how much better to let Him have first place in the morning so that my perspective starts out in agreement with His.

If we were to read further in Psalm 5, we would find that David trusted God to clear his path for the day. As a king, I am sure David was tempted to entertain sleepless nights as he worried about how circumstances and situations would turn out. He had great responsibility on his shoulders. There were enemy nations that wanted to overtake Israel and enemies within looking for ways to take over the throne. Some of those were members of his own household. Could he trust those around him to obey his commands? Was he making the right decisions based on what God would have him do? Was he a strong enough leader? Does he have what it takes to fulfill his position?

Isn't it an amazing thought that the God of the Universe is interested in your day? That He sees right where you are and knows how to clear your path. He knows what you need when you need it. All He is looking for is that we recognize our dependency on Him and meet with Him in prayer. I don't know about you–but that gives me ample reason to get up and start my day off with my Father. Has this not been your norm? His mercies are new every morning!

Practical Application

Identify what your particular habits are that keep you from getting the proper amount of sleep. What are small habits you can begin to make that will help you correct your sleeping patterns?

Do you meet with God on a regular basis in the mornings? What are small habits you can begin to make that will lead you into habitual morning prayer with God? It's usually the small changes that help us reach our big goals. Father will help you in setting this routine. Ask for His help and watch what happens.

FIND
ME!

Real Emotions–Real Devotions | Lester Bailey

Modern Psalm 17: Our Daily Bread

"And my God will meet all your need according to His glorious riches in Christ."
Philippians 4:19, NIV

The trucks are coming, the semi's are here.
Red and blue, green and teal.

To bring us the goods we need to live,
purchase or buy, receive or give.

I thank You my God for Your provision,
though some of Your people look with derision
on what You provide.

I'm thankful for all things, small ones and great.
Clothes that I wear, food I just ate.

My breath is to thank You for that is Your due,
For just who You are, not just what You do.

Did you ever expect to go to the store and not be able to buy toilet paper in America? Neither did I. The experiences of this past season seem surreal at times. Our way of life has certainly changed. One thing we did learn: our dependency upon the freight system in our nation for the goods needed is easy to take for granted.

During shelter-in-place, we were still able to get most of what we needed (once the toilet paper started appearing on the shelves again). Amazon recorded the largest profit they have seen in their twenty-six-year existence. If you were like most, when you noticed the Amazon truck circling your neighborhood, you wondered if it was your day for delivery.

Father has given us a life that He wants us to enjoy. But, because of the abundance we have grown up with in this nation, we often equate happiness with material belongings. We fixate on what we don't have and spend our time in anxious pursuit of whatever we think we need believing it will be the thing that fills the longing inside. Listen, there is nothing wrong with setting goals and achieving them. We truly are better people when we are pursuing something of worth and value with all diligence. A strong work ethic makes for strong character.

But there is a different kind of pursuit that will leave you empty in the end–it's the pursuit of money, material things, or accomplishments in order to fill the place inside your soul that only God can fill. And here is the interesting thing, sometimes we think those pursuits are for God's glory, when in actuality they are not. We see that in the story of Cain and Able.

> *"Now Abel kept flocks, and Cain worked the soil. In the course of time, Cain brought some of the fruits of the soil as an offering to the Lord. And Abel also brought an offering–fat portions from some of the firstborn of his flock. The Lord looked with favor on Abel and his offering, but on Cain and his offering he did not look with favor. So, Cain was very angry, and his face was downcast.*
> *Genesis 4:2-5, NIV*

Now, it's not plainly spelled out in the Genesis account just why God did not accept Cain's offering. Both an animal sacrifice and a grain offering were pleasing to God. And, both men brought an offering to the Lord from the work of their own hands. The word used for offering in this portion of scripture is **minchah**. It means a gift, a tribute, an offering. It's used in a general sense so it can encompass any sort of offering.

Again, nothing displeasing so far in Cain actions. But the issue lies somewhere else–it lies within the true intent of the heart. Hebrews 11:4 gives us this explanation, *"By faith Abel offered to God a more acceptable sacrifice than Cain, through which he was commended as righteous, God commending him by accepting his gifts. And through his faith, though he died, he still speaks."*

Abel's offering was offered with a desire in his heart to worship God. Cain's offering was more of an outward show without any real desire to come before God in humility. He just presumed upon God's acceptance. But 2 Timothy 2:19, tells us, *"...God knows those who are His..."* And, then in Psalm 25:14, ESV, the Psalmist writes, *"The friendship of the Lord is for those who fear him, and he makes known to them his covenant."*

Our heavenly Father wants our lives to be rich and meaningful. As a matter of fact, that's what Jesus came to do–to give us abundant life (John 10:10). But that life cannot be had apart from faith in God. It will always come up short. Jesus taught us what true worship looks like. *"God is spirit, and those who worship him must worship in spirit and truth."* John 4:24, ESV. Cain's offering was religious in nature. He gave outward lip service to God but was far from honoring Him in his heart. Abel on the other hand wanted to please God from the depths of his soul.

Listen, the word tells us not to chase after everything the world chases. God knows what we have need of and He will richly provide us with what is necessary to have a fulfilled life (1 Timothy 6:17). The question is: Are we going to let Him have His rightful place as Savior, King, and Father in our hearts; or are we going to seek after the worlds solutions to fill the void? One leads to life and contentment, the other to brokenness and disappointment.

Don't you find it interesting that Abel still has a voice that brings honor to God, even though he is dead? Do you want that kind of voice? I do! *"Give praise to the LORD, proclaim his name; make known among the nations what he has done."* Psalm 105:1, NIV. Look at what one act of faith can do throughout eternity–it can make God known throughout the nations. Wow! What a sacrifice!

Practical Application

Look up Matthew 6:30-33. What do you feel you need at this time in your life that is lacking? Be honest with God. After you list these things, ask Holy Spirit to put them in perspective for you based on God's heart. What do you hear Him say?

Look up Psalm 33:18. Who does God look upon? What adjustments do you need to make in your own heart to turn His gaze toward you? (That means to walk in His favor).

FIND ME!

Modern Psalm 18: Peacemakers

"Above all, love each other deeply, because love covers over a multitude of sins."
1 Peter 4:8, NIV

*I am a jokester, I jab, quip, and pick
Don't really care whose feelings I nick.*

*I set forth a pitfall and then laugh with glee
Watching your struggle to set yourself free.*

*Keeping the focus on you not myself,
I wait to broadcast like a good little elf.*

*I've noticed most recent the pool of victims has dwindled,
Could that possibly be from the fires I've kindled?*

*And don't talk to her, she's just a snit.
And he barks at me like he's just been hit.*

*Pastor says "do unto others like you want to be treated
and greet others too like you'd like to be greeted."*

*Something inside agrees that is true,
Starting today, I'm acting anew.*

*Laughing with friends, avoiding the tat.
Building them up, not pounding them flat.*

Culture is shaped by common values and attitudes within a people group. This is true for families, churches, businesses, cities, regions, and nations. One's identity within that specified group is formed by whether or not they adhere to the cultural values of that particular group.

Language plays a large part in cultural development. If you speak the language, you can find your place in the culture with ease. If you don't, it's not simply a matter of clear communication, often there is another value system in play. The use of sarcasm is a prime example.

John Haiman, a linguist at Macalester College in St. Paul, Minnesota says this, "Sarcasm (in 21st century America) is practically the primary language in modern society." Katherine Rankin, a neuropsychologist at the University of California at San Francisco states, "People who don't understand sarcasm are immediately noticed. They're not getting it. They are not socially adept."

https://www.smithsonianmag.com/science-nature/the-science-of-sarcasm-yeah-right-25038/

The problem with sarcasm being the preferred mode of communication is that it is defined as something derogatory in nature. Oxford defines sarcasm as the use of irony to mock or convey contempt. In the Bible, the Greek root word is sarx or σάρξ. It means flesh; that which is to be cut away when growth in the Spirit takes place. If we want to establish a culture based on Biblical principles and maturity, it requires that our words build up and encourage others. That's a far cry from the sarcastic communication that fuels our modern language.

> *"We all stumble in many ways. If anyone is never at fault in what he says, he is a perfect man, able to control his whole body. When we put bits into the mouths of horses to make them obey us, we can guide the whole animal. Consider ships as well. Although they are so large and are driven by strong winds, they are steered by a very small rudder whenever the pilot is inclined. In the same way, the tongue is a small part of the body, but it boasts of great things. Consider how small a spark sets a forest ablaze. The tongue is a fire..."*
> James 3:2-6, BSB

This scripture in James is set in the context of being a Biblical teacher. James tells us not many should aspire to this position because the responsibility is great, and the work will be held to a higher standard. Why is the tongue addressed in this context? -Because a teacher uses words to instruct. The words he or she uses will set the culture of the group being instructed. And for Christians, the words we use should be counter-cultural to the ways of the world.

James ends this portion of scripture with this, *"Who is wise and understanding among you? Let him show it by his good conduct, by deeds done in the humility that comes from wisdom. But if you harbor bitter jealousy and selfish ambition in your hearts, do not boast in it or deny the truth. Such wisdom does not come from above, but is earthly, unspiritual, demonic. For where jealousy and selfish ambition exist, there will be disorder and every evil practice. But the wisdom from above is first of all pure, then peace-loving, gentle, accommodating, full of mercy and good fruit, impartial, and sincere. Peacemakers who sow in peace reap the fruit of righteousness."* James 3:13-18, BSB

Isn't that what Jesus said as well? *"Blessed are the peacemakers, for they will be called children of God."* Matthew 5:9, NIV. I had to learn this lesson. I can recall how verbally abrasive I was to those around me until it became apparent that some people just weren't around much anymore. But God is gracious.

I had brave friends who taught me what God's word said about peacemaking. Biblical culture is a place where people should find deep healing from the things the world has thrown their way. Much of the time, the arrows flung our direction are in the form of painful words that have punctured our hearts. Words are powerful! They have the ability to tear down or to build up.

My perspective changed immediately when I said "Yes!" to God and His ways when it came to controlling my tongue. My relationships deepened. I found that people needed a safe place to grow. Peacemakers are those who help facilitate peace in the hearts of people who have been the target of the devil's contempt and mockery–his sarcasm. We don't have to be put off by those who use brash words. Most of the time, that is a protective mechanism that shields people from pain. But we need to remember that we are to be counter-cultural to what has brought the damage to their hearts. The words we use will reveal the culture we embrace.

But hey, we all have to start somewhere! That loud, boisterous, in your face, abrasive person could very well be someone like me.

Practical Application

This is your time to assess your words. Do they reflect the culture of the world or the counter-culture of the Kingdom? It's not easy to tame the tongue! But it is the pathway to maturity. Write out your thoughts about where you are on this journey and where you would like to grow.

Come up with a plan of action to help you in the taming of your tongue. Maybe you need a change jar that you pay when you slip up. Maybe you need an accountability partner. Or maybe what motivates you is something completely different. I just know, without a plan of action, we often do not see the change we seek.

Modern Psalm 19: Abundant Life

"And I commend joy, for man has nothing better under the sun but to eat and drink and be joyful, for this will go with him in his toil through the day of his life that God has given him under the sun."

Ecclesiastes 8:15, ESV

The workday has ended
My toil here is done
Time for some food
Time for some fun!

Dinner, a movie
A game or some golf
Fishing or walking
Nearby or off.

Alone or with family
Friends or a group.
To ponder our actions
Or leave them aloof.

Even in this Lord
We give You praise
Lips filled with song
Honor we raise

To worship the One
Who sits on the throne.
To spend time with You
We are never alone.

We learn from an early age that in America we have the right to "pursue happiness." Have you ever stopped to ponder what that actually means? The Greek philosopher Aristotle believed that happiness is the result of a well-lived life. But he didn't believe that a well-lived life was attained through pleasure seeking or reputation. He taught that the pursuit of happiness could only be achieved as one lived a life that served others and built up society. President John Kennedy alluded to this when he addressed the idea of pursuing happiness. He is quoted as saying it means, "the full use of one's talents along the lines of excellence."

It is important to remember that as America was being shaped and molded, the ideas of the day championed the rights of the individual. Before this time frame, people were born into a class structure and only a privileged few could pursue their own interests. The ideas of freedom and liberty were new to the average person. And although we have grown up with the ability to strike out on our own and make our own way, we often do not understand the full implications of what it means to be free until that freedom is taken away.

> *"Jesus spoke to them using this illustration, but they didn't understand what He was telling them. He said to them again, 'Truly, truly I tell you, I am the gate for the sheep. All who came before Me were thieves and robbers, but the sheep did not listen to them. I am the gate. If anyone enters through Me, he will be saved. He will come in and go out and find pasture. The thief comes only to steal, kill, and destroy. I have come that they may have life and have it in all its fullness.*
> *John 10:6-10, ESV*

In Solomon's pursuit to define what it meant to live a good life, he came to the conclusion that learning to enjoy the life you have been given is key. Why do you think that is important? Because we will always battle difficulties, whether physical or spiritual, that want to impede upon our pursuit of happiness. This is the thief that Jesus speaks of in the Gospel of John. Because of sin, the ideas of peaceful society that allow for freedom of expression will always be challenged by those who do not have the best interest of others in mind. But in Christ, we are free to pursue the abundant life no matter our external circumstances.

Psalm 34:1, NKJV says, *"I will bless the LORD at all times; His praise shall continually be in my mouth."*

What Jesus offers, that philosophers, presidents, or earthly kings cannot, is true peace. When the Bible speaks of peace, it refers to a sense of wholeness and well-being inside of a person. It is an internal work done by the Holy Spirit. Certainly, when Biblical principles are adopted by a group of people that community flourishes. But even if truth is rejected by society, we as individuals, can have abundant life in Christ. We can commune with the peace-giver Himself and learn to be conduits of that peace that surpasses all understanding.

I've learned a continual ongoing conversation with the Lord makes my interaction with people less stressful and curbs any attitudinal tendencies. Recently, I walked past someone from my office and was asked if my smiling was a result of it being a Friday. I hadn't realized that I was smiling. It's the tangible presence of the Lord that makes peace known.

Jesus told His disciples to bless the homes they entered. If a person of peace lived there, peace would rest in that home. If not, peace would return to the disciples. (Luke 10:6).

God's peace changes the atmosphere. Praising the Lord continually brings Him near. The ability to live in a free society and pursue dreams and opportunities is a blessing that should not be taken lightly. Jesus Himself taught us to serve others with the gifts we have been given. But we cannot fully achieve that until we appropriate the abundance of peace that Jesus wants to bring into our souls. Freedom is just that–a soul liberated from the tyranny of sin. And Jesus is no respecter of persons. It does not matter what class structure you find you are born into. The Gospel message is for you! All you have to do is enter the sheepfold through the gate–the person of Jesus Christ.

Practical Application

Take time to assess your dreams. Do you feel as though you are pursuing that which God has called you to do? Your divine purpose will be defined throughout your walk with God. However, one sure way of knowing if you are pursuing God's heart, or your own imaginations, is to ask this question. Are you offering up your gifts and talents to Jesus in prayer and asking Him to use them for His glory? It will certainly include community life in the sheep pen. We are at our best when we are fully surrendered to the Holy Spirit and serving others with what has been entrusted to us.

List out any changes you need to make in order to pursue happiness God's way.

FIND
ME...

Modern Psalm 20: Compassion

"Which of these three do you think was a neighbor to the man who fell into the hands of robbers? The expert in the law replied, "The one who had mercy on him." Jesus told him, "Go and do likewise."
Luke 10:36-37, NIV

Do you see one who is down
A smile has turned to frown?

Situation or circumstances amiss,
Feeling helpless like dangling over an abyss?

Take a lesson from "The Book" we read
of a Samaritan on a donkey not worried about speed.

To pick one up and not hold back,
To bandage the wounds and care for the lack.

Don't just look or pass on by,
Get off that donkey and give it a try.

God has blessed you, and now it's your mission
To stretch out a hand and fill "the commission."

So, none are left hungry, hurting or scared,
Alone without hope, no cupboards left bare.

But just help the one, don't look at the line,
The world can be changed one at a time.

Fear, loss, disease, financial struggle, and relational issues certainly have been heightened in our world. These things are not new, but because of the spiritual climate we find ourselves in, we don't have to look very far to find someone who needs our help.

It's easy to be sympathetic toward others who are in need. But sympathy alone is not what we are called to as Christians. Some of us are highly empathetic when it comes to feeling the struggles of the people around us. Empathy helps us relate to those who are hurting, but if not coupled with genuine love and concern, it can also cause us to shrink back so as to not be emotionally overwhelmed by the pain we sense.

As Christians, we are called to move beyond sympathy (pity for the suffering of others) and empathy (the sharing of emotions and understanding about suffering with another). We are called to have the same heart as Jesus. When Jesus saw those who were suffering, He had compassion on them.

> *"And when Jesus went out He saw a great multitude; and He was moved with compassion for them and healed their sick.*
> *Matthew 14:14, NKJV*

Miriam Webster's dictionary defines compassion as: sympathetic consciousness of another's distress with a desire to alleviate it. The Greek word used for "moved with compassion" in Mathew 14 has an even stronger connotation. It's the word ***splagchnizomai.*** The cleaned up version is that Jesus felt sorrow in His most inward being toward those who were sick, and it moved Him toward action. The literal meaning is to be moved in one's bowels, heart, lungs, and kidneys. In ancient Greece, these inward parts were thought to be the seat of love, affection, and pity. With this in mind, when Jesus was moved with compassion, He felt deep sorrow in His physical body for those who were sick, and it moved Him to alleviate their pain.

When we spend time with God in prayer, we get to know His heart. As Holy Spirit takes up residence within us, we begin to act in accordance with God's ways. Religion will make us cold toward others and we won't even realize it. When we are religious, we work so hard at being right with God that it makes us view others through the lens of fear or anger. We see other people as a hindrance to our spiritual progress instead of through the eyes of compassion. This has been a struggle for God's people throughout history. In the scriptures below, we see God's response to His people through the prophet Isaiah. They were good at fasting and observing the outward requirements of the law. But their hearts had grown cold. They trusted in their outward appearance of worship and had forgotten that true worship changes us and makes us true representatives of God's heart to those in need.

> *"Is not this the kind of fasting I have chosen:*
> *to loose the chains of injustice*
> *and untie the cords of the yoke,*
> *to set the oppressed free*
> *and break every yoke?*
> *Is it not to share your food with the hungry*
> *and to provide the poor wanderer with shelter—*
> *when you see the naked, to clothe them,*
> *and not to turn away from your own flesh and blood?*
> *Then your light will break forth like the dawn,*
> *and your healing will quickly appear;*
> *then your righteousness will go before you,*
> *and the glory of the Lord will be your rear guard.*
> *Then you will call, and the Lord will answer;*
> *you will cry for help, and he will say: Here am I.*
> *"If you do away with the yoke of oppression,*
> *with the pointing finger and malicious talk,*
> *and if you spend yourselves on behalf of the hungry*
> *and satisfy the needs of the oppressed,*
> *then your light will rise in the darkness,*
> *and your night will become like the noonday."*
> *Isaiah 58:6-10, NIV*

It's easy to ask superficial questions in which we really don't want to know the answer. "How are you?" "Are you doing okay?" "Are things good for you?"

We are prone to check the box for being cordial and continue on with our perpetual busyness. But coming out of this season of unrest and uncertainty, let's be more intentional in seeing the people around us and examine our motives. The questions may be exactly the same, but our willingness to follow up on the possible response could make all the difference for someone else.

Practical Application

The Good Samaritan story in Luke 10:30-36 gives some insight in changing the situation for someone else if we are willing to put forth the effort. The giving of our time, effort, and money could easily change the course of someone else's life and show the love of Jesus in a difficult situation. List some spiritual attributes, or some physical belongings you have that might be a blessing to others.

Pray and ask God to allow you to experience genuine compassion this week. Make a list of the kinds of situations in which you empathize with others. Look for those situations around you and ask God to help you have His heart in the matter.

FIND ME!

Psalm 21: Calling

"In the same way, let your light shine before others, that they may see your good deeds and glorify your Father in heaven."
Matthew 5:16, NIV

The neighbors are watching,
They peep through the blinds.
They watch what I do in front or behind.

The neighbors are watching
As I wash the car.
I could go to town, but that's just too far.

The neighbors are watching,
As I cook out back,
Play with the dog or feed the cat.

I know they are watching,
I don't mind if they see,
The fresh made cookies we took to Mrs. Lee.

Mr. Karnes is diabetic, so he gets some fruit.
Mr. Jenkins looks tattered, so we gave him a suit.

We helped weed the flowers in Mrs. Pearson's yard.
The Jergen's are sick, and we took them a card.

The neighbors are watching,
So, we're sure they'll see,
The Jesus inside us as we meet their needs.

Every person who knows Jesus has a specific calling on their life. We are given spiritual gifts that align with our Kingdom assignment. The truth is, we were created with this assignment in mind. What you are called into, fits you perfectly. However, in our modern Christian culture, we tend to view our calling as church work while we see everything else in our lives as a means to an end. In other words, we tend to think like this, "I need to work in order to make a living. But what I really want to do is serve Jesus."

In his book entitled The Call: Finding and Fulfilling God's Purpose for your Life, OS Guinness says, "Followers of Christ live by faith alone to the glory of God. There is no sacred vs secular, higher vs lower, perfect vs permitted, contemplation vs action where calling is concerned. Calling equalizes even the distinctions between clergy and laypeople. It is a matter of everyone, everywhere, and in everything, living life in response to God's summons."

We can say this was certainly true for Jesus. There were no distinctions in Jesus's life. When He was at a wedding, his mother asked Him to meet a need and He did. He taught heavenly principles as He met with His friends for dinner. He demonstrated the supernatural elements of the Kingdom as He moved from town to town. Yes, He pulled away to pray, but He also engaged the crowds. In everything Jesus did, He was simply about His Father's business.

> *"On one occasion, while the crowd was pressing in on Him to hear the word of God, He (Jesus) was standing by the lake of Gennesaret, and He saw two boats by the lake, but the fishermen had gone out of them and were washing their nets. Getting into one of the boats, which was Simon's, He asked him to put out a little from the land. And He sat down and taught the people from the boat. And when He had finished speaking, He said to Simon, 'Put out into the deep and let down your nets for a catch.' And Simon answered, 'Master, we toiled all night and took nothing! But at your word I will let down the nets.' And when they had done this, they enclosed a large number of fish, and their nets were breaking."*
> *Luke 5:1-6, ESV*

This of course is the dramatic way that Jesus called Simon Peter into discipleship. And we love the ensuing verse that says, *"From now on I will make you fishers of men."* (Luke 5:10). But that verse only makes sense in the context of Peter's vocation as a fisherman. And can you imagine what the other fishermen who were present experienced that day? At the end of their ordinary workday, they witnessed what could only be a genuine miracle. Don't think for one moment that the fishing community didn't talk that story up to everyone they knew. And where did Peter encounter Jesus? –on his job.

Whether you realize it or not, you make an impression on everyone you know–passive acquaintances, work relationships, distant friends, close friends, and certainly family. We should be people who are about the Father's business in every sphere of life. Our words and actions reflect our relationship with Him. When we are motivated by love, our words and actions towards others reflect God's heart back to those in our path. We shouldn't just put on our church face every Sunday and not take the reality of the Gospel into the other arenas of our lives. People are watching, let them see Jesus at work through you.

Jesus gave His disciples a charge to fulfill when He appeared after His death and resurrection. We know this charge as the Great Commission, *"Go therefore and make disciples of all nations, baptizing them in the name of the Father, the Son, and the Holy Spirit, teaching them to observe all that I have commanded you. And behold, I am with you always to the end of the age."* Matthew 28:19-20, ESV

No doubt, there are those who are called to lead large crusades into other nations. But as disciples of Jesus, these words ring true for each and every one of us. However, here is the great thing about this commission: The Greek word used for "go" is ***poreuomai***. It means having gone, or as you are going. So, in your daily life, as you go about your activities, make disciples of those around you. Nations are made up of people. Each individual has to come to a saving knowledge of Jesus for themselves. But as we rightly represent Jesus to everyone, everywhere, and in everything, disciples are made, first of individuals, then of people groups, then of entire nations.

Your calling and your work go hand in hand. OS Guinness reminds us, "Jesus was not a religious leader, but Lord of all life." He also says this, "In the second century, Christian apologist Justin Martyr grew up over the hill from Galilee. Interestingly, he notes that the plows made by Joseph and Jesus were still being used widely in his day. How intriguing to think of Jesus's plow rather than his cross–to wonder what it was that made his plows and yokes last and stand out."

Practical Application

Our words show others the reality of our hearts. Look up Luke 6:45. When people listen to you talk, what impression are you leaving them? Write out a short prayer telling Father that you want your words to honor Him at all times.

Our actions are motivated by our faith. Look up James 2:18. How can you walk in a deeper sense of your calling in your everyday life, showing others the reality of Jesus?

FIND ME

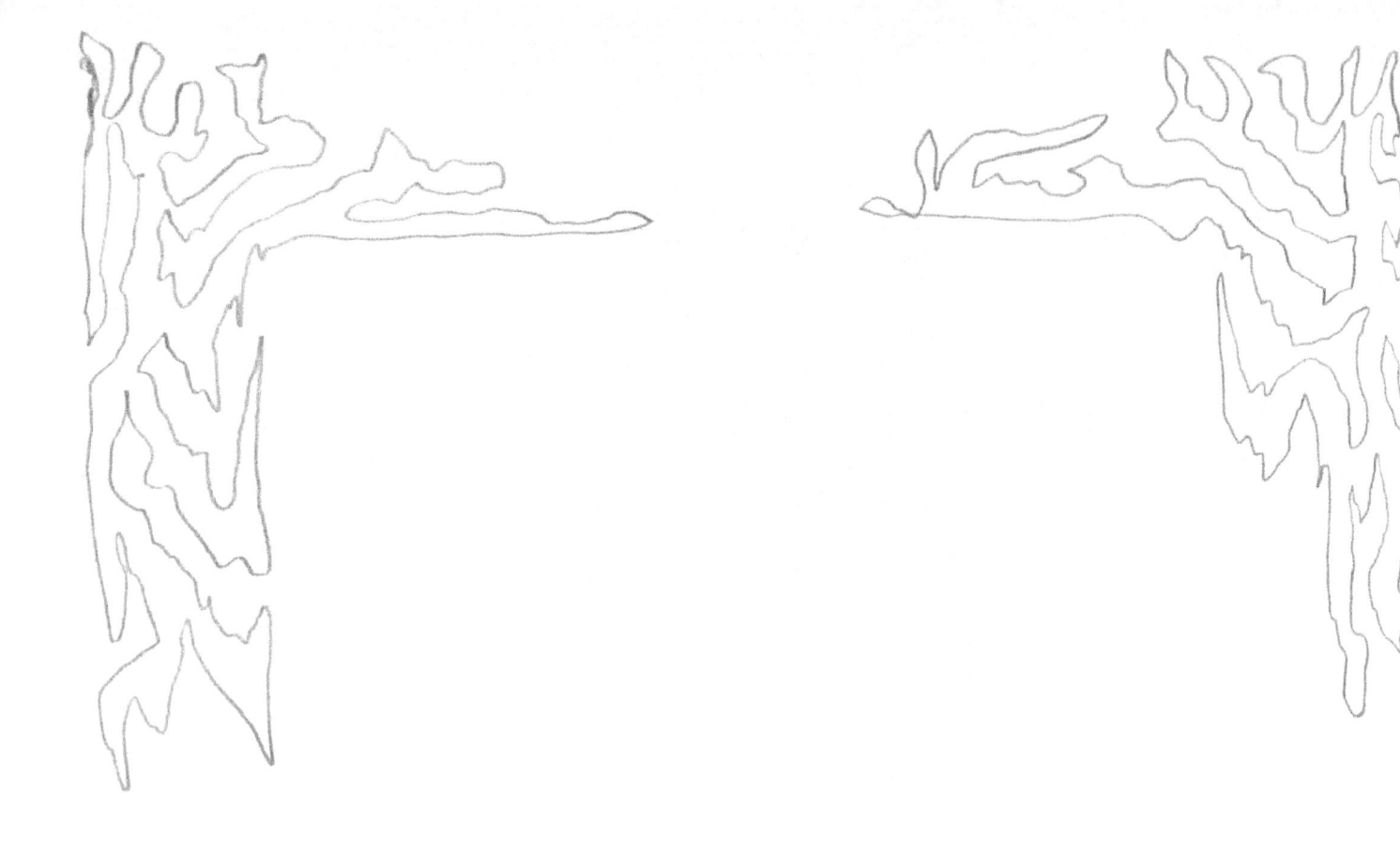

JONAH 4

ALWAYS TAKE
TIME to STOP
AND APPRECIATE
THE THINGS
GOD
HAS PROVIDED...

Modern Psalm 22: Honor

"Remind them to be submissive to rulers and authorities, to be obedient, to be ready for every good work."
Titus 3:1, ESV

That decision is stupid!
I know they can see
The frustration boiling up inside of me.

My ideas are perfect, and if they would hear,
Everyone's day would be full of cheer.

The birds would be singing,
The skies would be clear,
No one around us would shed any tear.

I am just right, and that answers that,
but mulling inside I hear a chat.

Holy Spirit whispers deep in my heart,
To honor authority, that's where we start.

The attitude's next and then stop the tongue,
Soon then I notice the battle is won.

Anger proves nothing, ranting feeds strife,
We are each called to only speak life.

Ground can be stood, just answer with peace,
Don't enter to argue, Let the truth speak.

The idea of submission is not a popular one these days. It summons up thoughts that seem antiquated and controlling in our modern mind. However, Biblical principles are true throughout the ages. These principles are a guiding light in our day, not to confine us to something outdated, but to help us live in the freedom that is ours in Christ. By learning to submit to those in authority over us, we partner with the Holy Spirit in our maturation process. Submission and humility go hand in hand. Our tendency to balk against authority is actually an effect of the fall.

What was the one thing Satan wanted that caused his downfall? –he wanted to be God. He wanted to be the captain of his own ship, the master of his own fate, the one who had all the answers and the one to be worshipped. He wasn't happy with the position he was given. He wanted more and he was willing to stand against his own Creator in order to get it.

In truth, a lack of submission in a person's life is an indication of a heart that will not be mastered. We call that rebellion. A rebellious heart usually blames everyone else for their troubles but is actually the cause of their own self-destruction. They will not be mastered; therefore, they cannot find true freedom. 2 Corinthians 3:17, NIV, says, *"Now the Lord is the Spirit, and where the Spirit of the Lord is, there is freedom."*

> *"But the fruit of the Spirit is love, joy, peace, forbearance, kindness, gentleness, and self-control. Against such things there is no law."*
> *Galatians 5:22-23, NIV*

Isn't it gracious of God, that once we are saved, He fill us with His Spirit so that we might live according to the principles of the Kingdom. When we cultivate this fruit that the Holy Spirit produces within us, we cannot help but walk in humility and submission. To do otherwise would mean that we choose to partner with the ways of the flesh and the world. And we simply do not belong to the worlds system anymore. We may have seasons where we find ourselves giving into the world around us, but it will never satisfy. We actually want to be mastered–by our loving Father. And that means, we must live counter-culturally to what is around us.

It's easy to question authority when the narrow scope of my personal views are all I can see. It is tempting to give voice to the idea that "things would be so much easier if done my way." But, truthfully, there is often a specific reason a task needs to be accomplished a certain way. Maybe for legal reasons I don't understand or to satisfy some accounting criteria. God calls us to respect authority because Paul tells us in Romans 13:1, ESV, *"Let every person be subject to the governing authorities. For there is no authority except from God, and those that exist have been instituted by God."* Parents also are set in place by God. We are told in Exodus 20:12, *"Honor your father and your mother, that your days may be long in the land that the LORD your God is giving you."* We see it again in the New Testament. Ephesians 6:1-3 says, *"Children, obey your parents in the Lord, for this is right. Honor your father and mother–which is the first commandment with a promise–so that it may go well with you and that you may enjoy long life on the earth."*

Continuing to read in Ephesians we find, *"Slaves, obey your earthly masters with respect and fear, and with sincerity of heart, just as you would obey Christ. Obey them not only to win their favor when their eye is on you, but as slaves of Christ."* Ephesians 6:5-6, NIV. We are not slaves, but this idea translates into the workplace. We should honor those in authority over us and work as we were doing the job for the glory of God. Because in essence, we are. That's the beautiful message submission speaks to all those around us. It shows that we live according to a different set of principles–one that transcends the world's system. By doing so, we honor our heavenly Father by showing Him that we trust Him to bring about what is needed to live well and enjoy the life He has given us. It also says to those in our sphere of influence that there is another Kingdom. One where the King is good; and deserving of our honor and submission. Because He is honorable, we live in step with His nature, and we are also honorable–even when it is difficult to honor.

Certainly, there is something to be said about how to handle situations that are abusive and damaging. That's for another lesson. But Paul spends much time on the principle of submission culminating in, *"Do not be overcome by evil (rebellion) but overcome evil with good (entrusting yourself to God and doing what is right).* Romans 12:21, NIV. We do this through following the Holy Spirit's lead. *"When the Spirit of truth comes, He will guide you into all truth, for He will not speak on His own authority, but whatever He hears He will speak, and He will declare to you the things to come."* John 16:13, ESV

Practical Application

Take some time to evaluate the relationships in your life. Would you say you are submissive to those in authority over you? –your parents, your boss, your pastor, etc. Ask the Holy Spirit to search your heart and show you anything that does not line up to His definition of submission. Write out anything you need to work on.

We are all in a growing process. That will be continual until we stand before the Lord made complete in His sight. You need the ministry of the Holy Spirit to grow you into the mature person you were created to become. Ask Him to cultivate the fruit of the Spirit in your life. Which fruit do you think you need the most help cultivating?

Modern Psalm 23: Living Water

"But God has revealed them to us through His Spirit. For the Spirit searches all things, yes, the deep things of God."
1 Corinthians 2:10, BSB

I sit by the well, the artesian well,
Not knowing where it starts.
I watch the water flow,
I know You have set this apart.
Creation shows Your greatness,
The sunrise is Your art,
I yearn to know Your deepest thoughts,
To share with you my heart.

The earth wells up the crystal flow.
So too my heart expels,
The deep that calls to deep
To know just where Your Spirit dwells.

The waters flow.
So too I know Your mercy ever swells,
To bring us life so much
Like the water from the well.
The seeming endless flow of grace extends to us to tell,
Of blessings, triumphs, and roads we've traveled,
Your goodness to propel.

A quiet moment to reflect
brings inner strength and healing,
The calmness in my spirit
You Yourself bring the revealing.
The deeper calm, much like a balm that draws me closer still,
To a new place, in Your grace, I will not repeal.
My hunger grows each time I spend the time I know so well,
To speak with You,
I find in places much like this one

the well...

Artesian wells are a fairly rare occurrence. The official definition of an artesian well is: 1. a well in which water is under pressure, especially one in which the water flows to the surface naturally. 2: a deep well.

The word artesian comes from the town of Artois in France, the old Roman city of Artesium. This is where the best known flowing artesian wells were drilled in the Middle Ages. It is common to call deep wells drilled into rock to intersect the water table and that reach far below it artesian wells. But this is not necessarily a correct use of the term. Deep wells may also be ordinary wells. Great depth alone does not automatically make them artesian wells. The word artesian, properly used, refers to situations where the water is confined under pressure below layers of relatively impermeable rock.

https://www.usgs.gov/special-topic/water-science-school/science/artesian-water-and-artesian-wells?qt-science_center_objects=0#qt-science_center_objects

Natural artesian wells do occur. Picture an underground river coursing miles below the surface of the ground that suddenly bursts into view and begins a surface waterway that services both plants and animals alike. Isn't it awe inspiring the way God created and set nature into motion.

We often look at the story of the woman at the well to show that Jesus went after those who society had deemed damaged or unclean. Or maybe we highlight the way He used the gifts of the Spirit to expose her need of Him. Both are correct, but there is another application that needs to be considered.

> *"A woman from Samaria came to draw water. Jesus said to her, 'Give me a drink.' The Samaritan woman said to Him, 'How is it that you, a Jew, ask for a drink from me, a woman of Samaria?' Jesus answered her, 'If you knew the gift of God, and who it is saying to you, "Give me a drink," you would have asked Him, and He would have given you living water.' The woman said to Him, 'Sir, you have nothing to draw with, and the well is deep. Where do you get that living water? Are you greater than our father Jacob? He gave us the well and drank from it himself, as did his sons and his livestock.' Jesus said to her, 'Everyone who drinks of the water that I give him will never be thirsty again. The water that I give him will become in him a spring of water welling up to eternal life.'"*
> *John 4:7-14, ESV*

Not only do we see the way God created nature as something to behold, but the spiritual wonders of God are also awe inspiring. Psalm 42:7, BSB says, *"Deep calls to deep in the roar of Your waterfalls; all your breakers and waves have rolled over me."* There is a thirst that only God can quench deep within the heart of all men. The deepest part of our being calls out to the deep things of God to know Him in a way that can only be accessed by the yearnings of our spirit in fellowship with His. Time spent in the deep well of God's presence intensifies the internal hunger to be closer to Abba Father. But this experience can only be had through a relationship with the One who is true living water–Jesus!

Do you see what Jesus actually gave this woman who had been discarded over and over again by those who used her and left her abandoned and shunned? He gave her deep intimacy with God. He gave her a sense of belonging she had never known. In the Old Testament, the Prophet Jeremiah tells the Israelites, that they have forsaken the spring of living water, and have dug cisterns of their own that cannot hold what they need (Jeremiah 2:13). And then again, he says, *"O LORD, the hope of Israel, all who forsake you shall be put to shame; those who turn away from you shall be written in the earth, for they have forsaken the LORD, the fountain of living water."* Jeremiah 17:13, ESV

But in the town of Samaria, the very place where the Jews would not go because they believed the people to be unclean–this woman, who was certainly a sinner–finds the very thing her soul is in need of–intimacy and love. Here the source of life itself–the Living Water who Jeremiah spoke of–says that once this Water is tasted, it will create a spring that will continually well up on the inside of everyone who drinks. The depth of her heart would no longer be a deep cavern of pain–she would house the very presence of God. Deep would call out to deep and get answered!

I would be negligent if we got to the end of this devotional, and I didn't ask you this question–Do you truly know Jesus? Have you drunk of the Living Water that quenches the deep heart thirst of your soul? All you have to do is ask Him for a drink–He will come gushing in to wash every stain and fill every crevice of your being.

All you need to do is come to the well with cup in hand. He will do the rest.

Practical Application

Take some time to truly evaluate your relationship with Jesus. Does His presence spring up like a fountain within you, or do you just go through the motions of religious activity? Write out the truth of where you are with Christ.

No matter the nature of your relationship with God, we should always be thirsting for more of Him. Write out a prayer that says just that…and then pray it.

FIND ME!

Modern Psalm 24: Fruitfulness

"So then, as we have opportunity, let us do good to everyone, and especially to those who are of the household of faith."
Galatians 6:10, ESV

Sitting in the fast food waiting for my turn,
Looking through the window to see what I can learn.

The lady that's behind looks a little stressed,
Kids are bouncing off the walls, she appears to be a mess.

The pickup truck in front is whooping at the girls,
Walking down the street out there shaking out their curls.

Somewhere back behind I hear the thumping of the bass,
They could be more considerate but that is not the case.

I ask the Lord for guidance to share with some His love,
And He sends a directive I'm sure is from above.

My turn is at the window now and so is set in motion,
The gracious act of kindness I'm sure is His notion.

"Allow me please to buy the next order," I asked the clerk,
The question was bewildering and was answered with a smirk.

The manager, assistant, and some came from the back,
To simply answer a question of the purchase next in fact.

The deed is now completed as I move ahead in space,
Bewilderment continues by the look upon her face.

I realize the gesture touched more than the intent,
Seen by those who helped contribute by handing thru the fence.

I thank you Lord for purpose and blessings meant to share,
And a moment just to listen and to pass on that You care.

- A mom of a six-year-old autistic boy held a birthday party for her son. No one showed up for his birthday. The mom let that be known on social media. Within the hour, over ten firefighters took it upon themselves to bring presents and attend this boy's party.

- When a New Yorker learned that a toy store was going bankrupt, she bought the store. She then donated all the toys to children living in foster care.

- Overhearing teenagers making fun of an elderly man's run-down house, a railroad inspector asked for help to paint the outside. Ninety-five volunteers showed up to paint the house and bring it back to life.

https://brightside.me/article/12-heart-warming-acts-of-kindness-that-changed-the-world-for-the-better-54455/

In the New Testament, the Greek word for kindness is ***chréstotés***. This word refers to meeting real needs, God's way; or Spirit-produced goodness which meets the need and avoids human harshness (cruelty).

This beautiful fruit of kindness is produced through the empowerment of the Holy Spirit in our lives. Certainly, lost people can choose to act in a kind manner. But we as people in general are not consistent in our kindness. That's why it's so important to cultivate the fruit of the Spirit.

> *"But the fruit of the Spirit is love, joy, peace, patience, kindness, goodness, faithfulness, gentleness, and self-control. Against these things there is no law."*
> *Galatians 5:22-23, NIV*

We no longer live under the letter of the Old Covenant Law that seems strict and impossible. We now are governed by the Law of the Spirit–the nature of the Kingdom that is shown through the fruit it produces in our lives. Kindness is only one aspect, but an important one.

Paul tells us in 2 Corinthians 3:17, NIV, *"Now the Lord is the Spirit, and where the Spirit of the Lord is, there is freedom."* This is an internal freedom to walk in a manner worthy of the Kingdom. Trying to live up to the Law of God through self-effort will only produce a religious way of life that never reaches its goal. Highly religious people have a difficult time being kind to others because they are not internally kind to themselves. They are always berating themselves for not measuring up. This perfectionistic view of how they relate to God transfers outwardly to others as they view people through a narrow lens of imperfection.

But being led by the Spirit means that I have discernment when it comes to other people. I see them through the eyes of their Maker. I see clearly the condition they are in, but I also see what God wants to bring about on their behalf and I seek to be a conduit of that blessing. That's why Paul also said, *"Or do you presume on the riches of his kindness and forbearance and patience, not knowing that God's kindness is meant to lead you to repentance?"* Romans 2:4, ESV

The best way to make a big difference where you are, is to do what you can when the opportunity presents itself. An ongoing conversation with the Lord will not only bring you closer to Him, but His presence in your life will make an impact in the lives of those around you. Something as simple as paying for the next order in a drive-thru may spark something in their heart that the Lord can use. It's just a few bucks, but the effort may change someone's perspective and open the door for the Lord to work.

Random acts of kindness display the best that collective humanity has to offer. But, for Christians, when we are led by the Spirit to do something kind, it is always so that Jesus might be on display. *"In the same way, let your light shine before others, so that they may see your good works and give glory to your Father who is in heaven."* Matthew 5:16, NIV

We are all called to be witnesses of the wonders of the Kingdom and the eternal Lordship of Jesus. The three examples given at the beginning of this devotional are even more powerful if done through the Holy Spirit and Jesus is brought into the picture. We can rightly represent Him to everyone we meet by being kind, joyful, and meeting a need, God's way.

Just be who you are, where you are; and let the reality of Jesus be seen through you. By doing that, your life will be a brilliant light that brings glory to the Father. And that is what abundant life is all about.

Practical Application

List again the different fruit of the Spirit. Pray and ask God to show you which of these He wants to cultivate in your life right now.

Now write out practical ways this fruit will look as it is produced in your life. Ask God to make this fruit available to others through your actions and attitudes. Be blessed in your adventure!

ALWAYS TAKE TIME TO APPRECIATE THE THINGS GOD HAS PROVIDED....

About the Author

Lester Bailey grew up in a rural central Texas community loving the outdoors, sports and church. Creative as a singer, musician, sound tech, actor and set designer, Lester's talents opened several doors of ministry. As a bit of a wit, poems became a trademark of holiday gift clues for the family and special events.

Lester has been married to his wife Sandy for forty-one years. They have three grown children.

A passing comment from the pastor one Sunday morning about writing a book sparked a barrage of verses that culminated in the writing of Real Emotions, Real Devotions: *Modern Psalms*.

Come share the range of emotions and the introspective journey that leads back to the Father. A journey that seeks to bridge the gap from where we are and where the Father desires us to be.

Thank you

You've reached the end of Volume 1. I pray some of my life experience in verse has broadened and/or deepened your perspective of how much our Heavenly Father cares and watches over us. I believe the most accurate description of His care is found in Jeremiah 29:11 (NIV), *"For I know the plans I have for you," declares the Lord, "plans to prosper you and not to harm you, plans to give you hope and a future."*

If you have enjoyed this devotional, please feel free to read through it again or pass it along to someone else. Volume 2 is in the works, and I appreciate your spreading the message of who Jesus is to those you have contact with on a regular basis.

If you're wondering about the recurring palm tree, it began as a cute doodle that I've taken as a logo of sorts. I usually reference Jonah 4. However, in stark contrast to what Jonah was feeling while overlooking Nineveh, I prefer being thankful for the things God gives me continually. The tagline I've penned to go along with it says, "Aways take the time to stop and appreciate the things that God has provided."

May every palm tree you see from this time forward cause you to remember just how much God cares for you!

Blessings ...

Made in United States
Orlando, FL
09 May 2022